Working with
TROUBLED YOUTH
in Schools

A Guide for All School Staff

Edited by
Garrett McAuliffe

BERGIN & GARVEY
Westport, Connecticut • London

Library of Congress Cataloging-in-Publication Data

Working with troubled youth in schools : a guide for all school staff / edited by Garrett McAuliffe.

    p. cm.
  Includes bibliographical references and index.
  ISBN 0–89789–853–2 (alk. paper)
   1. Youth with social disabilities—Education—United States. I. McAuliffe,
  Garrett.
  LC4091.W68 2002
  371.93—dc21   2001058320

British Library Cataloguing in Publication Data is available.

Library of Congress Catalog Card Number: 2001058320
ISBN: 0–89789–853–2

First published in 2002

Bergin & Garvey, 88 Post Road West, Westport, CT 06881
An imprint of Greenwood Publishing Group, Inc.
www.greenwood.com

Printed in the United States of America

The paper used in this book complies with the
Permanent Paper Standard issued by the National
Information Standards Organization (Z39.48–1984).

10 9 8 7 6 5 4 3 2 1

Dedicated to the dreams of Julio Rodriguez, Reggie Williams, and all their junior high school classmates from Brooklyn who brought me into their lives in 1974. You needed more than remedial reading. I needed to do more than to teach you to understand words. My work has never been the same.

Contents

Illustrations

Preface

With this volume, we culminate the work of three years, a time that we, the authors, have spent pondering, testing, challenging, and discovering what might work with troubled youth. In a sense, our work begins with this writing, for we ask you yourselves to implement these ideas and to tell us of their success. We have found them to be difficult but powerful. They are not ideas for the hackneyed school professional who is cynical, too tired, or biding time until retirement. They are for those who have fire in their eyes, whose light is internally generated from a moral urgency to "save souls." As I tell my classes of future counselors, this work is not for the fainthearted.

This book offers both a conceptual foundation for the work of helping troubled youth in schools and model programs for enacting such a vision. The topics range from the broad leadership work of school administrators to the moment-by-moment interactions with students. It is meant to be a guide for practicing school staff. It is intended to be either immediately useful or to be a stimulus for longer-range enactments. All chapters are written by veterans of "school work": individuals who themselves are or have been principals, special education directors, directors of guidance, school counselors, school psychologists, or school social workers. They know what of they speak. Their ideas have been tested in the fires of three highly interactive working conferences for practitioners and an ongoing series of public presentations to professional groups. These conferences were held for one academic year in order to generate solutions to the challenge of educating troubled youth.

Two sets of words echo throughout this book. They might go under the rubrics of "connect" and "prevent." The first encompasses such terms as "network," "linkage," "ecological," and "collaboration." It is a call to reduce isolation among professionals, between school staff and families, and among staff, families, and community members. The second cluster includes such words as "alertness," "socially critical," and "reaching out." It is a call for prevention and proactivity. Let these words be our constant companions in the work of helping troubled youth. We must remember: Their opposites are isolation and reaction. Those notions have already demonstrated their fatal consequences.

1

Conceptual Foundations for Work with Troubled Youth

1

1

Making the Circle Large: Enacting Intentional Efforts at Personal–Social Development through Schooling

Garrett McAuliffe

When a Methodist minister from California was asked how we might understand the two school shootings that had occurred in his county within a three-week span in the early months of 2001, he remarked pointedly, "The circle around those young people was small." The minister was reminding us of age-old wisdom from many cultures: Much of our strength lies in our community. It is a lesson that can easily forgotten by the individualistic, often laissez faire, lure of the American ethos (Bellah, 1985).

Most cases of school violence are characterized by some kind of social isolation. Yet all young people should be standing on the shoulders of giants: their families, neighborhoods, teachers, school counselors, coaches, and religious group members. All human beings owe much to the circle of community that is around us and behind us. However, the tendency in the dominant Anglo-American culture is to locate ultimate power in the individual. Such a "hyper-individualism," in sociologist Robert Bellah's (1985) words, is revealed in President George W. Bush's rationale for his choosing some ethnically and gender-diverse key Cabinet members: "These are just effective people who are qualified. They have made it by their own efforts. Period." Such a myth of hyper-individualism is common. It is also a convenient, and perhaps self-serving, myth for a male who is "from money" to believe in. And we can appreciate the political value of that statement—it increases the perception that these Cabinet members are talented and ambitious. That is good. But neither they nor any of us have "made it alone."

The price that we pay for our cultural hyper-individualism is high. In its extreme, it assigns the "losers" to the dust heap in which castoffs dwell. The sole location of power in the individual represents a tension that American society has not dealt well with, for we are not islands. Instead, our tentacles inevitably stretch, often unknown to us, into networks of human connection. This is the reminder that the minister is offering.

So let us widen the circle of community for all youth, especially those who are "troubled." Let it surround us all. That theme is conveyed in every chapter of this book. The authors hope that this volume is a reminder, a wake-up call, to bring the community to the lives of troubled youth. School staff can create such a world: arrangements that bring "askable adults" and supportive peers into the circle, arrangements that enhance the circle of community. Conversely, school staff can do the opposite: they can reinforce the single-minded pursuit of meritocracy that leaves the road littered with the "undercircled," and their victims.

SCHOOL VIOLENCE AS AN ALERT

Perhaps the only benefit of school violence is that it has drawn attention to the problem of troubled youth in schools. Perhaps violence attunes us to social problems that have been festering unnoticed, ones that cause immediate pain to individuals and long-range damage to society. Violence can thus be an alert for school professionals to heed those young people who are not doing well, who are being lost in systems that only pay attention to two ends of the spectrum: academic achievement and extreme dysfunction.

This volume is therefore not only "about" school violence, but it is also about troubled youth in all their manifestations—the 20% (Clark, this volume) who show mental disorder to a great enough extent to be labeled in the *Diagnostic and Statistical Manual of Mental Disorders*, or DSM (2000), some living in quiet desperation, others loudly calling attention to their struggle. It is about bridging the gap between the need and the community response. Let me quote the proceedings of the Surgeon General's 1999 Conference on Children's Mental Health:

A major study . . . has shown that schools are doing a very poor job of identifying children [who have mental health disorders of any kind], or at identifying them soon enough. Among thirteen-year-old children . . . diagnoses such as depression, attention deficit-hyperactivity disorder, and post-traumatic stress disorder secondary to abuse were made. Before these children got into special education, parents reported recognizing a problem at a mean age of 3.5. Outside agency records (e.g., discipline referral, prescription medication) indicated problems at a mean age of 5 (i.e., kindergarten), and the first documented intervention involving some sort of pre-intervention was at age 6.5. The first eligibility for special education was at about 7.8 years (i.e., toward the end of second grade), and in more than 50% of the cases, these children were placed in the category of LD, not ... ED. *These children finally got the right services at age 10.* (Italics mine)

Five years elapsed between agency recognition of problems and school services.

THE CENTRALITY OF PERSONAL-SOCIAL DEVELOPMENT IN THE SCHOOL CURRICULUM

The standards for this effort to attend to troubled youth are already in place: "Personal-social development" is at the present time one of the three supposedly equal spokes in the trinity of school counseling priorities. The other foci are, of course, "academic development" and "career development." We see these three standards as equal tasks of our profession, and of schooling in general. The star of "personal and social development" has variously risen and fallen in the past century, as trends and crises have drawn attention to the academic (e.g., the math-science response to Sputnik and the current academic testing movement), the career (e.g., the original vocational guidance impulse of the 1910s and the 1970s career education movement), and the personal/social (e.g., the juvenile delinquency scare of the 1950s and the substance abuse programs that were triggered by drug use in the 1960s). School staff responded to each of the previous personal-social "crises" with attention and resources. But consider the following report, as represented by Clark in this volume: Even though 90% of students believe that their teachers care about their academic growth, only 40% believe that those teachers care about their personal feelings and social problems. Perhaps our vigilance has slipped. Perhaps the sun of "academic accountability" and "standards of learning" has eclipsed the star of educating young people for personal-social development. This book offers a counter to such a dark and myopic vision. Every community and every culture throughout history must attend to young people's emotional and moral development, or suffer the consequences. Let us rally once again, as educators have in the past, around the cry for help that students broadcast, when they drift in storm-tossed waters, when they lack a career compass, when they are marooned in isolation, and when they anchor themselves to drugs, alcohol, or eating disorders. Let us re-anchor ourselves

in the ground of our forebears, like Frank Parsons, in the "social improvement" movements of the turn of the century. The star of educating young
people for moral and personal-social development can never set—it is our
chosen lot as educators to follow it, to enhance the normal development of
young people and to respond to the inevitably "abnormal" cataclysms that
many young persons are heir to.

Academic development is instead pushed almost exclusively, if I am
reading the legislation and the verbal reports of teachers, administrators,
and school counselors accurately. But personal-social development just
won't go away as a schooling issue. It "intrudes" on academic and career
progress in every era, for a large percentage of students. Only the most extreme elitist, or true-believing advocate of pure meritocracy, or suspicious
religious zealot would eliminate the role of school staff in actively enhancing students' personal-social development. Many young people need the
school community to supplement, even substitute for, the gaps in family
and community environments. From simple self-doubt and crises of confidence, through anxiety and depression, all the way to harm to self and others, the "felt life" clamors. It won't go away, even if many school
professionals would like it to. We ignore the cacaphony at our peril. So, this
book is an invitation to "bring in the noise," even if ironically, it takes the
form of silent desperation for some youth. Let us therefore, with
open-minded, "religious" fervor, be trinitarians all, toiling to unite the academic, the career, and the personal-social needs of young people.

THE PRICE OF IGNORING STUDENTS' EMOTIONAL
LIVES: A CASE

Let me share a personal anecdote, one that might be replayed many
times in the lives of our children, one that confronts educators with the
ethical question in regard to responding to young people's personal-social
development: If not us, who? If not now, when? Pay now or pay later. I did.

As an eight-year-old third grader, I was prone to moments of fear and distress when our class was detained in school beyond the normal release time
for some reason. I was exquisitely vigilant about the noon hour as it approached, the time to return to the safety and warmth of my home for
lunch. Anxiety first trickled, then flowed, then flooded me, as we were (often) kept in school beyond noon. The etiology of my condition, that of
childhood anxiety, is beyond our purpose here. The remediation, however,
is not.

One day, at a school assembly that was being held in the hard white light
of the church auditorium, our rehearsal for some event was running late.

The clock edged from noon to 12:01, and, minute by minute, to 12:10. The hot flash of panic burned in me, the internal drumbeat of "I won't get home, they forgot the time" thundered in my ears. I could barely stifle the growing tension and the pent-up tears at the delay. After enduring a tortuous ten minutes of growing distress, I finally burst into tears, causing a stir among my peers. It was then that Sister Maria Del Ray swirled toward our class, inquiring as to the matter. The auditorium fell silent. As her steel-gray eyes flashed at me, her crimson face as big as the room itself, I sobbed, "It's lunch time and we're supposed to be let out for lunch now." I still can feel the embarrassment, the shame, as she launched a salvo at me, a barrage of incriminations that I vaguely remember as, "How old are you? And a boy! You crybaby, you should be ashamed of yourself!" Her voice echoed across the silenced assembly. It went on.

The sting still lingers. I managed to plod through my childhood, enduring much shame for this fear, and considerable anxiety. Fear of disgrace was one of my companions: I might be found out as fearful. Would a kinder, more empathic response have changed much? Would a caring teacher or counselor have helped me to understand my plight and to manage it? Yes and no. In the 1960s we didn't know much about helping anxious children. We were all pretty much held to one standard of behavior, thought, and feeling. There were few, if any, "askable adults" in our schools. But my sense of inadequacy at being unable to "cope" lingered. My mistrust of authority figures (as all educators seemed to be) grew into major adolescent rebellion. With a caring teacher's or counselor's ear, I might have gained confidence to speak up about my fears rather than to hide them deeply in my psyche. The shame drove those fears to a preverbal level of awareness, and perhaps led to a defensive stance toward relationships and disclosure with peers and adults. I was one of the lucky ones who had an intact, loving extended family, an at-least lower middle-class environment, and a free public university to grow in.

And thus the educators whom I encountered in my youth failed. No, they taught spelling and arithmetic, and later poetry and algebra. But they failed to see individuals. They couldn't see the relationship between adult success and emotional development in childhood. They missed a chance to help a child who was suffering find some relief. And although the price was not fatal, it was high. Fifteen years of repression and hiding might have been avoided by a teacher's alert attention to a "troubled" child.

Sometimes all that is needed is an early alert and empathy to help a child in distress. Often more is required—limit-setting, challenges to change behavior, family consultations, social interventions, referrals, medication. Sometimes a whole system needs modification—who is placed in which classes, how children are taught, instigating team consultations, delivering preventive guidance. None of these were in place for me and my classmates. And there were other, greater casualties among my peers.

OUR HOPE AND PURPOSE: CONNECTION AND PREVENTION

This volume asks us to break the cycle of denial that surrounds psychosocial problems in youth, to open up the discussion, to "look for trouble." It does not ask for the school to become a mental health agency. But—let us be very clear—we do not back down from raising the standard of "personal/social development," in the American School Counseling Association's words, high, as a schooling responsibility, one that is equal to academic and career education.

Our book and our long-term commitment to working with troubled youth in schools aims at uncovering both innovations and reminders. Two major themes that run throughout this volume might be simply summarized as "connect" and "prevent." The first is a call to bring networks of stakeholders together—colleagues, parents, community members. The second is to pay attention, early and often, to the rumblings of both normal and abnormal child development.

We are not short on specific strategies for this effort. Participants in the surgeon general's Conference on Children's Mental Health (Department of Health and Human Services, 1999) offer three recommendations for practice. In the call for prevention, their words are consistent with the guidance offered by this volume:

(1) Train school professionals, especially classroom teachers, to recognize early symptoms of emotional and behavioral disorders, (2) Modify the school definition of mental health disorders, which is more restrictive than definitions for other school categories, and (3) Develop a more proactive identification process for mental health disorders in school, in which children are screened for emotional or behavioral disorders early in school years.

The document asks school staff to open up to the mental health dimension of education.

Such recommendations put a lot of responsibility onto "mere" educators, those whose focus must also be on academic achievement. It might be a relief therefore to hear the urgings of Dr. Velma LaPoint of Howard University, a presenter at that same conference. She reminds school staff to connect and prevent. To quote the Proceedings: "Dr. LaPoint advocates a holistic, ecological approach to children's mental health. . . . [She emphasizes] the need for professionals to *meaningfully and proactively involve families* in identifying children's mental health needs, and in developing, implementing, and evaluating interventions. . . . *A broad assessment of children's social competence, including their assets and support networks, is needed by educators*" (italics mine). Dr. LaPoint goes on to describe the particular power of school counseling in the effort, along with its current deficits (e.g., student-counselor ratios and noncounseling tasks). She further urges school staff to establish networks with social workers and nurses in order to create prevention and treatment programs for troubled youth (LaPoint, 2000).

There is also a social class issue at play here. It is often the families who are least able to address personal-social development who need schools to help. Otherwise, schools will remain the promoters and protectors of privilege; they will enhance environments for those who already have adequate personal and social development and support. Only the "strong" will survive, whoever they are. But "a society is only as strong as the weakest of its members," goes the axiom.

The charge is clear and the path is marked: Pay attention to children's personal-social development, do it proactively, and include many stakeholders from agency colleagues to families. We hope that within these pages are methods that respond to the call heard at the surgeon general's conference. Without innovations and reminders, such as those contained in this work, personal-social development will again recede in importance.

This book asks all school personnel to consider this urgency: Pay attention to the quietly anxious eight-year-old, to the sixteen-year-old isolate, to the socially isolated immigrant child, to the thirteen-year-old who is getting thinner before our eyes from her eating disorder. We already do much with these young people that is good. However, the authors in this volume fear that the gains of this century will be compromised by a narrower, even meaner, impulse that goes by the name of "academic accountability" or "standards of learning." School staff will be focused on drilling students on academic content. If these "standards" are totalized, the tripod will be left with only one leg—that of "academic development." Those with the additional props of family support and financial resources will be the ones left standing. The path will be littered with the casualties of this meritocracy. Without timely interventions that address personal and social development, the price for the needy child and to society will be high.

I know. I paid it.

REFERENCES

American Psychiatric Association Task Force on DSM-IV. (2000). *Diagnostic and statistical manual of mental disorders: DSM-IV-TR*. Washington, D.C.: American Psychiatric Association.

Bellah, R.N. (1985). *Habits of the heart: Individualism and commitment in American life*. Berkeley: University of California Press.

Department of Health and Human Services. (1999). *Report of the surgeon general's conference on children's mental health*. http://www.surgeongeneral. gov/cmh/childreport.htm.

LaPoint, V. (2000). *Report of the surgeon general's conference on children's mental health: A national action agenda*. Retrieved March 28, 2001 from http://www.surgeongeneral.gov/cmh/childreport.htm.

2

Academic and Behavioral Support for Troubled Youth: Time for the Twain to Meet

Alan A. Arroyo, Robert A. Gable, and George Selig

Schools throughout the nation face a myriad of "high-stakes" reform initiatives. Foremost among these initiatives is that schools must be accountable for achieving positive academic outcomes, as measured by student performance on various academic criteria or standards of learning. In many schools, the changing demographics of the student population pose particular challenges to accomplishing that goal. Because of diverse backgrounds and experiences, not every student comes to school ready to learn. More and more students evidence a mix of academic, social, and emotional needs (Arroyo, Rhoad, & Drew, 1999). In that most teacher preparation programs provide limited training in this area, most school personnel find it especially difficult to deal with those students who engage in various kinds of misbehavior.

There is growing recognition that most student misbehavior is linked to academic failure (Nelson, Scott, & Polsgrove, 1999). Today, many students experience only limited academic success—especially in the critical areas of reading and reading comprehension. Other students are unable to participate appropriately in instruction or to control their tempers. These problems often arise because students are improperly placed within the academic curriculum, exposed to ineffective classroom instruction, or subjected to inconsistent behavior management (Gable, McConnell, & Nelson, 1985;

Sheurermann, 2000). In addition, manageable classroom situations sometimes are exacerbated due to student academic difficulties, such as failure to
respond to academic requests, and to triggering teacher disciplinary actions,
such as office referrals (Skiba, Peterson, & Williams, 1997). In that mount-
ing evidence shows that learning and behavior problems go hand-in-hand
(e.g., Kauffman, 1997), it seems logical that schools simultaneously address
these two interrelated problems (Bullock & Gable, 2000).

Schools everywhere are looking for ways to respond to students who
manifest overlapping academic and behavior problems. Many schools are
introducing both schoolwide academic *and* behavioral supports to establish a more nurturing and effective learning environment for all students.
These schools are finding that an integrated approach to addressing academic and nonacademic instruction is an efficient way to respond to the diverse needs of troubled students (Gable et al., 1999). In the following
discussion, we highlight various supports that school personnel can introduce at the building and classroom level to address the academic and behavioral needs of troubled children and youth.

THE FAILURE OF REACTIVE APPROACHES

The accumulated research tells us that traditional "reactive responses"
to the problems of troubled children and youth, such as office referrals, detention, in-school/out-of-school suspension, and expulsion, have not
proven effective. Critics of current "zero tolerance" policies argue that
these largely punitive, authoritarian practices emphasize harsh punishment over responsible education (Civil Rights Project of Harvard University, 2000). Critics maintain that adhering to punitive disciplinary
practices alone may exacerbate the problem by accelerating the course of
antisocial and delinquent behavior and increasing the likelihood that students will drop out of school (e.g., Gable et al., 1999). Finally, critics claim
that simply removing the student from the regular classroom setting fails to
address the root cause(s) of the problem and does little to reintegrate the
student into the school or community as a better citizen. This evidence underscores the need for alternative approaches to remedying student learning and behavior problems.

WAYS TO PROVIDE ACADEMIC AND BEHAVIORAL
SUPPORTS TO ALL STUDENTS

Four programming ideas for addressing behavioral problems are described. They are the notion of schoolwide "academic and behavioral sup-

port teams," classroom-level programming, the use of functional behavioral assessments with troubled youth, and focused programming for especially troubled youth.

School-Based Academic and Behavior Support Teams

One alternative approach to dealing with learning and behavior problems that is being implemented in a growing number of schools is based on a team problem-solving process. Various school personnel are taught to function as a team to address schoolwide student issues. A major responsibility of the multidisciplinary team is to establish clear expectations for students, ones that apply throughout the school. In addition, the team crafts a schoolwide reinforcement plan (e.g., token economy, "group-individualized contracts") and a consistent discipline policy to address student behavior that violates these standards. In that way, it is possible for schools to create a coordinated, multi-tiered, school-based program that addresses the group-individual needs of all students. The multidisciplinary team may be comprised of general education and special education teachers, school counselors, school psychologists, and other support personnel, as well as parents and students.

A major characteristic of schoolwide support teams lies in the importance that these programs attach to individual differences in students as learners. Every student is afforded equal but not necessarily the same opportunities to succeed. Other distinguishing characteristics include the use of proven interventions that are appropriate to the context(s) in which the problem behavior occurs (e.g., classroom, cafeteria, corridor). Finally, emphasis is on achieving student academic and behavioral outcomes that meet community standards.

Classroom-Level Programming for All Students

Student misbehavior often is triggered by academic failure that results from poor classroom instruction. Given the diverse needs of students, teachers must strike a balance between establishing a predictable classroom routine and making timely adjustments to instruction (Arroyo, Rhoad, & Drew, 1999). Examples include the following:

1. A limited number of classroom expectations taught to students systematically (by means of modeling role play and corrective feedback) and situationally (at the time/setting in which the expectations apply)

2. The routine use of differentiated instruction (i.e., making curricular accommodations and/or instructional modifications that match student abilities and needs)
3. High levels of student academic engagement and correct responses
4. High rates of teacher praise of student achievement
5. Frequent teacher "out-of-seat" behavior, to increase physical proximity to students, increase the power of verbal and nonverbal praise, increase the opportunity to give immediate feedback, and to "troubleshoot" student academic performance (e.g., make immediate "repairs" in flawed student practices)

Together, these strategies have a "spread effect"on student performance, meaning the worth of each strategy is strengthened because of its connection with the others.

There are various ways to effectively deal with classroom management. Teachers have long recognized that certain classroom situations have the potential to become behavioral problems (e.g., when students make the transition from one instructional activity to another). By identifying potential problems *before* they take hold and become major impediments to the teaching/learning process, teachers can take immediate steps to remedy the situation. With this so-called "precorrection instruction," the teacher systematically manipulates various potentially significant classroom variables—teaching strategies and procedures, curricular content, instructional groupings, teacher expectations or demands, and ways students respond to instruction, to mention a few (Colvin, Sugai, & Patching, 1993). Then, the teacher carefully observes the effect of a change in classroom practices on particular students and makes additional instructional modifications, as the situation demands. Sometimes direct intervention is required to teach one or more students more appropriate or acceptable classroom behavior (e.g., having the student accept a delay in teacher acknowledgment of a correct response). Overall, an integrated program of schoolwide and classroom-level academic and behavioral strategies has been shown to be effective in addressing the behavior of about 90% of the school population (Conroy, Clark, Gable, & Fox, 1999). For those students who do not respond to these strategies, more focused interventions are required, which flow from what is known as functional behavioral assessment.

Use of Functional Behavioral Assessment with Troubled Youth

For more troubled students—about 7% to 9% of the student population—the multidisciplinary team establishes more complex and intrusive kinds of interventions (Conroy, Clark, Gable, & Fox, 1999). Usually these interventions stem from what is known as a functional behavioral assessment (FBA).[1] FBA is a team problem-solving process that allows educational personnel to find positive ways to decrease student misbehavior and to teach students more appropriate and socially acceptable alternative behavior. The introduction of FBA in schools was prompted by the 1997 Individuals with Disabilities Education Act (IDEA). This federal legislation requires that school personnel work collaboratively to address student misbehavior that seriously impedes the teaching and learning process and that is serious enough to evoke disciplinary action.

Conducting a Functional Assessment

In conducting a functional behavioral assessment, a multidisciplinary team collects various kinds of information on both the problem behavior of the student(s) and on the social, academic, and physical context(s) in which it occurs (e.g., history class, school cafeteria). In some cases, information gathering can be accomplished informally and in a short amount of time because the reasons behind the misbehavior are self-evident (e.g., Larry acts out in reading class because he lacks the skills to respond correctly to teacher requests).

When either the law or the complexity of the problem demands a formal FBA, the team meets to identify the behavior(s) of concern and to develop an initial course of action. Ordinarily, information-gathering tasks are divided among team members. One person may be asked to review the accumulated school records for information about the student's problem(s), whereas another might conduct a series of structured interviews with adults who have direct knowledge of the student (e.g., teachers, school psychologist, guidance counselors, and parents). In most cases, the student of concern is interviewed as well. At the same time, one or more team members usually engage in a series of direct observations in both the settings in which problem behavior occurs both more often *and* least often—such as in English and geography classes versus American history class. The roles and responsibilities of team members may vary according to both prior preparation and experience and the exact stage of the FBA process. In that no two students likely misbehave for the same reasons, no two functional assessments likely will yield the same kind or amount of information.

With the knowledge gleaned from multiple sources of information, the team attempts to identify the reason (or reasons) behind the misbehavior. Many times, the team will find that student misconduct serves at least one of three functions: (1) to gain attention (e.g., peer approval, teacher recognition, or both); (2) to avoid or escape an aversive situation (e.g., a boring or too-difficult assignment, a negative peer interaction); or (3) to communicate a need (e.g., control of a social conflict). The team uses that information to develop an intervention plan to promote a replacement behavior that accomplishes the same purpose, that is, serves the same function for the student, but is more socially acceptable. Based upon the functional behavioral assessment and an analysis of all the information collected, the team makes a "best guess" regarding the motivation behind the behavior.

Next, the team develops a plan of intervention, evaluates the fidelity or faithfulness with which it is carried out, and assesses its actual impact on student behavior. The positive behavioral intervention plan and supports usually include strategies and procedures that address the "learning process," in order to remedy student skill and/or motivational deficits that are behind the problem. For example, any teacher can be taught to systematically instruct students in appropriate ways to request assistance on a difficult assignment; the guidance counselor might bring in a series of structured lessons and role-play activities on conflict resolution among classmates; a special education teacher or school psychologist might teach students self-regulation strategies to control anger and frustration. Regardless of the strategy, experience has shown that skill building strategies are most effective when they are (1) linked to the motivation behind the misbehavior, and (2) carried out in the setting(s) in which the new skill (replacement behavior) will be applied (e.g., world history or geography class, school cafeteria or auditorium).

Focused Programming for Troubled Youth

The remaining 1% to 3% of the student population poses the most serious behavior problems. These are the students who have received the highest number of office referrals, incident reports, and the most in-school or out-of-school suspensions. For these students, a positive behavioral intervention plan is developed following a functional behavioral assessment and may include an emergency/crisis component as well (Gable et al., 1999). In some cases, the plan is completed in cooperation with representatives of outside agencies (e.g., community mental health, juvenile justice). In the end, there is a commitment to more longitudinal intervention plans that are more complex and intrusive in nature. They may include anger management and self-control training, social skills instruction, critical thinking/problem-solving training, receptive and/or expressive language therapy, conflict resolution instruction, and/or crisis management.

CONCLUSION

Throughout the United States, administrators, teachers, parents, and students are concerned about problem behavior in the schools. Many experts agree that we have the knowledge to deal successfully with most difficult behavior; the implementation problem lies in putting what we know into the proper context. We have here proposed that schools place emphasis on prevention and early intervention of learning and behavior problems by incorporating functional behavioral assessment into a larger organizational framework of positive academic and behavioral supports. In that way, educational personnel are able to prevent and eliminate most problems and to create a safe and effective learning environment for all students. To do such prevention and early intervention requires a fundamental shift in educators' thinking about the nature of student behavior problems and the relationship between student behavior and classroom performance. It also requires strong administrative and faculty commitment, combined with a high quality program of in-service training and ongoing technical support. The payoff is clear: few would question whether the commitment of time, energy, and resources required for establishing systems of positive academic and behavioral supports is too great a price to achieve the goal of preventing behavioral and learning problems.

NOTE

1. Readers who are interested in learning more about functional behavioral assessment can obtain an informational booklet entitled "An Overview of Functional Behavioral Assessment and Behavioral Intervention Plans in Virginia's Schools," from the Virginia Department of Education; call (804) 225–2709. More detailed information is available through the Center for Effective Collaboration and Practice, Washington, DC; (888) 457–1551 or center@air.org; www.air.org/cecp.

REFERENCES

Arroyo, A.A., Rhoad, R., & Drew, P. (1999). Meeting diverse student needs in urban schools: Research-based recommendations for school personnel. *Preventing School Failure, 43*, 145–152.

Bullock, L.M., & Gable, R.A. (Eds.) (2000). *Positive academic and behavioral supports: Creating safe, effective, and nurturing schools for all students.* Reston, VA: Council for Children with Behavioral Disorders.

Civil Rights Project of Harvard University (July, 2000). *Opportunities suspended: The devastating consequences of zero tolerance and school discipline policies.* Cambridge, MA: Harvard University.

Colvin, G., Sugai, G., & Patching, B. (1993). Precorrection: An instructional approach for managing predictable problem behaviors. *Intervention in the School and Clinic, 28,* 143–150.

Conroy, M., Clark, D., Gable, R.A., & Fox, J.J. (1999). Building competence in the use of functional behavioral assessment. *Preventing School Failure, 43,* 140–144.

Gable, R.A., McConnell, S., & Nelson, C.M. (1985). The learning-to-fail phenomenon as an obstacle to mainstreaming children with behavioral disorders. In R.B. Rutherford Jr. (Ed.), *Monograph in behavioral disorders* (pp. 19–26). Reston, VA: Council for Children with Behavioral Disorders.

Gable, R.A., Quinn, M.M., Rutherford, R.B. Jr., Howell, K., & Hoffman, K. (1999). *Addressing student problem behavior—Part II: Conducting a functional behavioral assessment.* Washington, DC: American Institute for Research.

Kauffman, J.M. (1997). *Characteristics of emotional and behavioral disorders of children and youth* (6th ed.). Columbus, OH: Merrill.

Nelson, C.M., Scott, T., & Polsgrove, L. (1999). *Perspective on emotional/behavioral disorders: Assumptions and their implications for education and treatment.* Reston, VA: Council for Children with Behavioral Disorders.

Sheurermann, B. (2000). Curricular and instructional recommendations for creating safe, effective, and nurturing school environments for all students. In L.M. Bullock & R.A. Gable (Eds.), *Positive academic and behavioral supports: Creating safe, effective, and nurturing schools for all students* (pp. 7–10). Reston, VA: Council for Children with Behavioral Disorders.

Skiba, R., Peterson, R.L., & Williams, T. (1997). Office referrals and suspensions: Disciplinary intervention in middle schools. *Education and Treatment of Children, 20,* 335–346.

3

Reaching Potentially Violent Youth in Schools: A Guide to Collaborative Assessment, Alertness, Atmosphere, and Accountability

Mary Ann Clark

A CHANGING WORLD

"The times they are a-changing." These words from Bob Dylan's song of a generation ago are as true today as they were then. People seem to be busier. They have a difficult time jumping off of their treadmills. Technology has changed the way people communicate with one another, for better or for worse. More parents are working longer hours and children seem to grow up more quickly, whether or not they are ready for it. The schools and other societal institutions exist in an age of accountability, where citizens are asking for tangible results. This inquiry produces greater pressures on educators and students.

In this postmodern environment, young people have more freedom and rights, but don't always exercise the accompanying responsibilities, although it should be noted that many do. School violence has been on the rise for a while. Data reported by the National Center of Educational Statistics revealed that the number of students victimized rose by nearly 25% from 1989 to 1995 (Sandhu & Aspy, 2000). Teens themselves are victims of crime more frequently than any other age group (Moone, 1994) Many students fear for their own safety. Weapons are much more accessible. Indeed, there are almost as many guns as people in the United States. Gun control is a powerful controversy, as more and more people seem to possess them and feel a need to protect themselves and their families. Others cannot conscience easy access to guns.

At the same time, most U.S. citizens are reeling from the tragic violent incidents of the past few years that have taken place in our schools, resulting in the loss of students' and educators' lives. What can educators do about it? Many feel a strong sense of frustration as they see the statistics relating to school violence, and wonder how they can transform the world into being a safer place.

Some attempted solutions are obvious. Visible signs both of how things have changed over the last ten years and of the attempts at solution, which include the presence of police officers in schools, metal detectors through which students must walk when they enter their buildings, security cameras in the hallways, mandatory student and staff identification cards, and locked doors for which visitors must receive permission to enter. Although many of these issues are related to larger societal problems, they are manifested in the schools. A dilemma for many educators is that they are trained to teach and guide young people; they do not perceive themselves to be police officers or mental health workers.

What can educators specifically do to help students and parents feel that schools are the safe havens that they would like them to be? This chapter explores major dimensions of preventing and responding to school violence. In particular, effective strategies are organized into "four A's" of violence prevention, namely, "assessment" of potential violence, "alertness" to potential violence, the "atmosphere" for preventing violence, and shared "accountability" for preventing and responding to violence. In particular, shared responsibility on this issue among six stakeholders will be emphasized.

ASSESSING POTENTIAL VIOLENCE

Early assessment is hard to do but essential to preventing many cases of school violence. There is much to assess, and many tools available for doing so. In the general area of mental health, approximately 22% of children and adolescents have difficulties that need treatment (National Advisory Mental Health Council, 1990, as cited in Callahan, 2000). In particular, oppositional defiant disorder and conduct disorder have escalated. They exemplify the anger, antisocial behavior, and acting out that an increasing number of young people are manifesting (Lyman, 1996). Recent analyses of elementary and middle school disciplinary referral patterns indicate that 6% to 9% of children account for over 50% of the total number of discipline referrals and virtually all of the major offenses, such as assault (Skiba, Peterson, & Williams, 1997, as cited in Sprague & Walker, 2000).

In contrast to the extent of the problem, less than one-fifth of youth who exhibit mental health difficulties receive the help they need (Costello, 1990; Tuma, 1989; Zill & Schoenborn, 1990, as cited in Callahan, 2000). Steven Hyman, director of the National Institute of Mental Health (NIMH), blames that gap on the continuing stigma associated with mental illness. This absence of care is not related to treatment failure: 80% to 90% of people who are treated for a mental health problem increase their ability to lead healthy, productive lives (Simmons, 2000a). One task is clear: school staff need to be vigilant about the warning signs of antisocial behavior and must actively respond to them.

The "Who" of Assessment: Shared Responsibility for Problem Identification

It is not only the counselor's job to target these problems. For example, the FBI's recently published profile of potentially violent youth identifies three groups of school staff, namely counselors, teachers, and administrators, who share responsibility for preventing violence (Simmons, 2000a). This profile provides a four-part assessment system that school staff might use to identify children and adolescents who may be on the edge of violent behavior.

In the schools, educators are the primary professionals who are responsible for early assessment of potential violence in the schools, even though mental health and law enforcement professionals also have roles. All educators, whether they are teachers, administrators, or counselors, need to be able to identify those youth who are exhibiting signs of depression, anger, withdrawal, and drastic changes in behavior. Although violent behavior can be difficult to predict, there are a number of warning signs of which educators need to be aware.

The "What" of Assessment: A Guide to the Warning Signs of Potential Violence

In response to violent incidents in schools, concerned adults, including educators, parents, neighbors, and friends, have usually asked themselves a series of disturbing questions: Why didn't we see it coming? What could we have done differently to prevent this horrible occurrence? Why didn't the police act on the information they had? Why didn't the school personnel get wind of the problems the students were having? How could parents not see what was going on in their own homes? Didn't the kids' friends have any idea of what was going on in the minds of their peers? Would stricter rules and curfews have made a difference? and What can we do to make sure it doesn't happen again?

The Difficulty of Assessing Potential Violence

For many youths who acted violently, hindsight indicated that there had been a noticeable buildup to the acting out. They seemed to be operating from some suppressed anger, either at authority figures, peers who had rejected them, or parents. However, some seemed to just explode over a seemingly minor incident, as in the case of the middle school boy who was angry at having been suspended from school for the first time, and returned to school to shoot a teacher. All had access to lethal weapons.

Demographic Clues

It is difficult to make generalizations and come up with a profile to predict violent behavior. We do see a few commonalities, however, when we examine the high-profile incidents that have taken place in recent years in American schools. For example, most often the perpetrators are male. However, girls have participated in or planned a small percentage of attacks. Most of the extreme violent incidents that have attracted the attention of the media have taken place in middle and high schools, although the age range has spanned from elementary through high school. The majority of the attackers have been from middle-class suburban homes, and most have been white. An examination of their pasts reveals that some of the students had histories of discipline problems, but that others did not.

Warning Signs

With so few valid generalizations to draw from, other than the "male-adolescent-anger-and-available-lethal-weapon" matrix, the identification of students who may engage in dangerous behavior becomes very difficult. However, there are warning signs of potential violence. School staff need to be aware of these indicators and help others to be vigilant about them as well. Warning signs include:

- Social withdrawal, especially if it is a change in behavior
- The expression of excessive feelings of rejection
- Becoming increasingly upset about being teased or bullied
- Impulsive and chronic hitting or bullying
- Increase in alcohol or drug usage

- Personality changes (e.g., a student who has become moodier, is acting out angrily, or is showing severe mood swings)
- Intolerance for differences, especially those regarding race, ethnic group, and sexual orientation
- Access to weapons
- A strong interest in violence, as shown by choice of movies, music, video games, and a fascination with weapons
- Expressing violent feelings through writings and drawings
- Demonstrating uncontrolled anger in response to what the average person may call minor irritations

Additional cues lie in affirmative responses to the following questions. School staff should ask, "Does the student state threats?" and "Has the student personally been a victim of violence?" (as the previously victimized student is more at risk of turning violence on others).

Criteria for Evaluating the Warning Signs

After noting the warning signs described earlier, the school staff member should apply the following criteria in order to determine whether an indicator is out of the normal range (Myrick, 1997):

Frequency—How often does this behavior occur? For example, has a student "picked on" another student just once or twice, or is his bullying behavior chronic?

Duration—How long has it been going on? Has the student been exhibiting the behavior over a period of time, and is it getting worse?

Intensity—How intense is the student's behavior or expression of emotion? Are angry feelings acted out with aggressive behaviors toward others, such as fighting or threatening with weapons?

Affect—Are the emotions expressed appropriate to the situation? For example, does the student show remorse? Does he or she laugh when tears may be more appropriate? When a perpetrator commits an aggressive act, does he or she show any guilt, shame, or a sense of being wrong? Or does the student act like it was his or her right to behave in such a way, showing little feeling of empathy for others?

ALERTNESS: ACTIONS TO TAKE IN PREVENTING VIOLENCE

It's Okay to Tell: Reporting as Prevention

One of the main problems with regard to incidents of school violence has been the lack of communication about worrisome student behavior. In a number of cases, people have had strong regrets about not telling another adult about suspicious or inappropriate behavior. It is now known that in all of the national incidents of school killings someone knew about what the students were planning but didn't share it with school police or officials (Kennedy, 1999; Barras & Lyman, 2000). Counselors may have worried about confidentiality, teachers may have brushed off disturbing student remarks, or parents may have dismissed warning signs with, "It's a stage he's going through." Fellow students may not have wanted to "rat" on their friends; they may have experienced fears of retaliation (Barras & Lyman, 2000).

Parents, teachers, and students should be encouraged to report suspicious behavior to counselors, administrators, or others who can help. Police officers, who are in many schools, can also be important allies. The lesson is this clear: If someone is contemplating doing harm to self or others, it needs to be told; warning signs should not be ignored. Confidentiality is not an issue in such a circumstance. All need to work together to protect one another. There have been a number of recent situations where students or teachers have reported suspicious behaviors and threats and have thus helped avert a potential disaster.

THE ATMOSPHERE FOR PREVENTING VIOLENCE

A Positive Approach to the Prevention of School Violence

The broader long-range picture of school atmosphere plays a large part in preventing violence, even though responses to specific immediate threats of violence are obviously crucial. An optimal school environment is needed, one in which students have hope, ambition for achievement, goals, and a sense of planning for the future.

The National Center for Student Aspirations (NCSA) found in a national survey that 90% of students believe that teachers are concerned about their academic growth. However, in contrast, only 40% believe that teachers care about their personal and social problems and feelings (Quaglia, 2000). These student perceptions likely reflect the pressure on teachers that have been created by increasingly tough educational standards and assessment measures (Dodd, 2000; Arroyo, Gable, & Selig, this volume; Quaglia, 2000).

The NCSA report asserts that certain conditions need to be in place to promote student aspirations in schools nationwide. The underlying assumption is that if students feel cared about, they won't act out so much. These conditions represent a significant change in the focus of schools. They stand for a positive, global approach to violence prevention. The conditions that students need are listed below, followed by the attendant task of school staff to ensure their establishment.

A sense of belonging: Establish a sense of community and participation and believe that students are valuable members of that community.

Sense of accomplishment: Recognize and appreciate effort, perseverance, citizenship, and the learning of more than subject matter, as well as academic achievement.

Heroes (sometimes called "Askable Adults"): Have a caring adult in the school that each student can feel personally connected to, to whom they can turn for advice and can trust.

Curiosity and creativity: Allow and encourage students to question and explore, and to keep this inquisitiveness ignited through the teenage years.

Spirit of adventure: Support students in their taking healthy chances; let them know it is all right to try and fail, as well as to succeed; and provide students with the opportunity to understand consequences, as well as benefits.

Fun and excitement: Provide an interesting and enjoyable learning experience that communicates that it is okay to have fun while learning.

Leadership and responsibility: Give every student a voice in the learning environment, and let them know that they matter and are responsible for their decisions.

Self-confidence: Encourage students to believe in themselves, to believe that they can be successful and make a difference; help them to be comfortable and assured in their personal and emotional growth.

SHARED ACCOUNTABILITY FOR PREVENTING AND RESPONDING TO VIOLENCE

Accountable Parties in Violence Prevention Work

Who is responsible for assessing, alerting, and creating an optimal school atmosphere, one that will create a safer school environment? Each of the following parties must play a part: administrators, counselors, teachers, students, parents, and community members. They can collaborate in various combinations to create and enact interventions such as "Zero Tolerance Programs" (in which aggressive, harassing, bullying behavior is not allowed in the school), peer mediation programs, crisis intervention guides, and antiharassment policies. All these programs must communicate the message that all parties will work together for a safe school. Toward this end, a network of people who will collaborate in reaching the goal of school safety should be formed. The roles of each of the six parties to violence prevention is discussed below.

The Role of the Administrator

The priority for administrators is to set a tone that the school is a safe place to be. The administrator of an effective school will help to establish a positive school climate where students and staff feel listened to, valued, and respected by each other. The effective administrator will make sure that the school is a positive place for all students to be. He or she will stress safety issues and will reiterate the policies that safeguard the school. The leader will ensure that all participants know the roles and responsibilities that they are to carry out.

The general responsibilities of administrators can be broken into specific tasks. For example, the principal and assistants must enforce appropriate and consistent consequences for offenders. That is, they will make sure that staff and students know what the expectations are, as well as what are the disciplinary measures for those who break the rules. Beyond the school building, effective administrators must foster community connections and encourage parent involvement. In the building, they must be visible in the classrooms, hallways, cafeteria, and extracurricular activities in order to support counselors and teachers in their efforts to send safety and antiviolence messages. Administrators can also show leadership by providing release time and resources for in-service training on the issues of safe schools and violence prevention.

The Role of the School Counselor

The counselor should be a partner with the administrators in this effort. They can share the leadership role on a "school safety team." Such a team can identify specific school needs, specify safe school goals, and develop and implement safe school plans. In the area of prevention, the counselor can help to establish a network of people who might identify students who are at risk for mental health problems and potentially dangerous behavior. The counselor can also be a co-creator of "postincident reaction interventions" by collaborating on a school crisis plan with other team members from the school and the community. The purpose of such a plan is to have guidelines and helpers in place for the time when a crisis might occur.

In the broader developmental arena, school counselors can help students to address the normal crises of growing up. They can plan and implement classroom guidance activities for a K–12 curriculum. The counselor can promote character, citizenship, anger management, problem solving, and prosocial skills. All these interventions can help students contribute to the safer school environment. School counselors can educate teachers, parents, and students about the warning signs of school violence and can encourage them to alert others to potential problems.

The Role of the Teacher

Teachers are the cornerstone of a caring and respectful school environment. They have the greatest amount of contact with students. Teachers should be vigilant to students' concerns. They should report worrisome behavior to one or all of three different types of persons, depending on the circumstances: administrators, counselors, and parents. Teachers can hold classroom discussions on safety and violence issues and follow up on a counselor's guidance sessions. Allowing students to express their views and concerns about these issues and giving them information can make the issues public. Through such discussions students will be encouraged to report any potential problems to adults in the school.

Teachers can learn to be "behavior watchers." They should record their personal observations in the classroom and on the playground, perhaps using rating forms for adaptive and maladaptive behavior (Sprague & Walker, 2000). In this way, they can help screen potential offenders by referrals to counselors and administrators. They should not tolerate bullying or harassing behavior in their classrooms.

The Role of Parents

Research shows that parental involvement is correlated with increases in academic achievement, higher test scores, improved attendance, and more positive attitudes toward school (see Dorries, this volume). Parents can encourage their children to talk about their feelings, be aware of their children's friends and activities, and become more involved with their children's school. They should be encouraged to communicate with the school about their children (see Scaringello, this volume). If parents have concerns about their children, they need to talk to the teachers and the school counselor to help resolve the issue. It is important for parents to support and reinforce school rules and regulations, and to ask for help with their children when it is needed.

The Role of Students

Students need to be aware of their responsibilities, as well as their rights. They should be held accountable for upholding school rules, for themselves and for others. Students can be key in helping to maintain a caring and respectful school environment. They can consistently attempt to engage in positive communication with their peers and the adults in the school. Further, they can demonstrate moral action by standing up for others who may be victimized. Finally, they should tell a school adult if another's actions and words seem suspicious.

The Role of the Community

Community members can provide a large blanket of support for the schools within their boundaries. First, they can provide support for the missions of the schools by gathering and providing supplemental funding for special projects or materials that may go beyond the school budget. For example, many businesses are interested in having partnerships with schools in which the business contributes materials or financial support to a particular endeavor. A bank can provide scholarships for students in need.

Money is only one way in which community members can supplement the work of school professionals. Increased adult involvement can result in students having positive role models. Community members can do volunteer work in the schools and increase their visibility as interested adults and mentors to students. Businesses can provide release time for their people to spend time in the local schools where they can provide extra help, for example through tutoring (see Taylor and McAuliffe, this volume).

A school-community planning team can be very helpful in launching collaborative programs relating to school safety and violence prevention. Such a team should include school staff, parents, and students, as well as representatives from law enforcement organizations, community mental health agencies, the faith community, local businesses, local government, and other community-based service providers (Cunningham & Sandhu, 2000).

CONCLUSION: A TEAM APPROACH TO PREVENTING SCHOOL VIOLENCE

Many stakeholders can join together to forge a safety network in schools, one that might ensure the physical and emotional security and safety of our students and ourselves. It is important to see our roles as overlapping one another. Counselors, administrators, teachers, and parents all wear a number of "hats," as they share in counseling, teaching, disciplining, and leadership tasks. Such teamwork is essential; in isolation much less is accomplished than can be done by an interdisciplinary team with the same purpose. For example, for a counselor to have a successful program it is vital to have the principal's support. And for the principal to run an effective school, an involved guidance and counseling staff is essential. The mission is the same: to help students do the best they can do in their academic, social, and emotional lives. By forming a supportive network and safety net and being vigilant to students' feelings, behavior, and concerns, we can help students thrive in a safe and stimulating environment.

REFERENCES

Barras, B., & Lyman, S.A. (2000). Silence of the lambs: How can we get students to report pending violence? *Education, 120* (3), 495–502.

Callahan, C. (2000, March). *The counselor's role in safe schools: An administrative and counselor paradigm shift.* Paper presented at American Counseling Association conference, Washington, DC.

Costello, E.J. (1990). Child psychiatric epidemiology: Implications for clinical research and practice. In B.B. Lahey & A.E. Kazdin (Eds.), *Advances in clinical child psychology* (vol. 13, pp. 53–90). New York: Plenum.

Cunningham, N.J., & Sandhu, D.S. (2000). A comprehensive approach to school-community violence prevention. *Professional School Counseling, 4* (2), 126–133.

Dodd, A. (2000). Making schools safe for all students: Why schools need to teach more than the 3 R's. *NASSP Bulletin, 84* (614), 25–31.

Kennedy, M. (1999). The changing face of school violence. *American School and University, 71* (11), SS6 (3).

Lyman, D. (1996). Early identification of chronic offenders: Who is the fledgling psychopath? *Psychological Bulletin, 120,* 209–234.

Moone, J. (1994). *Juvenile victimization, 1987–1992: Fact sheet #17.* Washington, DC: U.S. Department of Juvenile Justice and Delinquency Program.

Myrick, R.D. (1997). *Developmental guidance and counseling: A practical approach* (3rd ed.). Minneapolis, MN: Educational Media Corporation.

National Advisory Mental Health Council (1990). *National plan for research on child and adolescent mental disorders* (Report No. NIMH 90–163). Rockville, MD: National Institute of Mental Health.

Quaglia, R.J. (2000). Making an impact on student aspirations: A positive approach to school violence. *NASSP Bulletin, 84,* 614, 56–60.

Sandhu, D.S., & Aspy, C.B. (2000, May/June). Violence in American schools. *The ASCA Counselor, 21.*

Simmons, J. (2000a, October). FBI releases study aimed at identifying dangerous students. *Counseling Today, 43* (4), 1.

Simmons, J. (2000b, October). Kids' mental health tackled. *Counseling Today, 43* (4), 1, 26.

Skiba, R., Peterson, R.L., & Williams, T. (1997). Office referrals and suspensions: Disciplinary intervention in middle schools. *Education and Treatment of Children, 20,* 335–346.

Sprague, J., & Walker, H. (2000). Early identification and intervention for youth with antisocial and violent behavior. *Exceptional Children, 66* (3), 367–379.

Tuma, J.M. (1989). Mental health services for children: The state of the art. *American Psychologist, 44,* 188–199.

Zill, N., & Schoenborn, C.A. (1990). Developmental, learning and emotional problems: Health of our nation's children, United States. *Advance data from vital and health statistics* (Report No. 190). Hyattsville, MD: National Center for Health Statistics.

4

The Dynamic Interaction between Students and the School Environment: An Ecological Approach to Aggression

Charles R. McAdams III and Victoria A. Foster

This chapter is inspired by a very real problem: the challenge of both preventing and coping with violence among youth. It is a response to the toll that violence takes on young people themselves and on all those family members, friends, educators, and professional service providers who have contact with them. The lost achievement, the legal consequences, and the pain associated with violent behavior can be devastating (Kazdin, 1993).

For professional educators themselves, student violence poses the obvious risk of personal physical harm. There is also evidence to suggest that the emotional impact of the event on educational and clinical service providers can be severe and have long-term consequences, whether or not there is physical injury (McAdams & Foster, 1999). In particular, the psychological and emotional impact of violence on the novice educator may be particularly critical (McAdams & Foster, 1999).

The topic of youth violence is not universally nor uniformly addressed in teacher preparation programs. The levels of attention given to the presence and needs of aggressive students may vary significantly within both formal education programs and in-service training curricula for different educational service settings. As a result, some teachers and administrators are neither adequately informed about the nature of violent behavior nor are they prepared to address it. Here we describe the interactive or "ecological" nature of youth aggression so that educators might know its face. Further, we propose a conceptual framework for educator preparation and practice regarding student violence.

UNDERSTANDING THE ECOLOGICAL NATURE OF AGGRESSION IN YOUTH

Although it is subject to a variety of individual and situational interpretations, violent behavior is generally defined as "aggressive behavior involving a threat or application of force and having the potential for physical damage or injury to others" (Monahan, 1984, p. 113). Most violent behavior appears to be "ecological" rather than individual in its origins and effects; that is, it appears to occur through a dynamic interaction between an individual and his or her environment and not as a result of either individual or environmental conditions in isolation. Individual characteristics such as mental illness, substance abuse, violent history, youthfulness, marital status, and association with antisocial peers all appear to predispose individuals to a higher probability of violence. However, these factors alone or in combination still cannot reliably predict its occurrence (Harris & Rice, 1997; Newhill, 1992).

Numerous efforts to explain and predict violence on the basis of individual personality or character traits have proven largely unsuccessful (Newhill, 1992). Equally unsuccessful have been research efforts to predictively attribute violence to individuals who have a psychiatric diagnosis or condition. For every study reporting a positive association between violence and such diagnoses as paranoia, mania, paranoid schizophrenia, panic, and antisocial personality disorder, there seems to be another reported poor association (Newhill, 1992).

Attempts to predict violent student behavior according to specific environmental conditions have also fallen short of their goals. When compared with the rates of violent behavior in the general population, the rates of violence among hospitalized and even incarcerated client groups are not significant (Harris & Rice, 1997). Thus, we cannot isolate either the individual or the environment in order to understand violent behavior. We can, however, connect the two in this way: the single most distinguishing commonality among violent individuals across the lifespan appears to lie in their perception of themselves in relation to their environment.

COGNITIVE CHARACTERISTICS OF AGGRESSIVE INDIVIDUALS

Violent individuals characteristically tend to share the following qualities. They (a) view themselves as weak, ineffectual, inadequate, and not in control of their environment; (b) see others as powerful and controlling; (c) feel vulnerable to loss of self-control to others; (d) view most stressors as cause for panic; and (e) perceive themselves to have low levels of family or other external support (Newhill, 1992). When they feel threatened by a real or imagined loss of power to control to their environment, individuals with these cognitive characteristics may be more likely to act aggressively on their world in an effort to reestablish a sense of self-control and personal competence. Although the above five characteristics fall short of being solid predictors, their prevalence among those who are violent underscores the significance of the person-environment relationship to violent behavior. This underlying "ecological" theme for violence can be further illustrated through examining five recurring patterns that have been observed in child and adolescent aggression.

PATTERNS OF AGGRESSION

Aggressive episodes characteristically occur in one of the five general types or patterns that are presented in Table 4.1: Overaroused, Impulsive, Affective, Predatory, and Instrumental (Hunt, 1993).

All but one, the overaroused pattern, appear to be manifestations of the preceding five cognitive characteristics. Overaroused aggression occurs simply as an unfocused physical expression of energy and excitement that is unintentional and largely unrelated to self-environment perception. The impulsive and affective patterns, on the other hand, are reactive and usually irrational responses to a disequilibrium of power that is perceived to exist between some individuals and their environments. Feeling powerless, vulnerable, and personally unsupported, such individuals are at an increased risk of becoming frustrated and angry and of acting impulsively and destructively on their emotions in an effort to reclaim some sense of personal control (Kaplan & Wheeler, 1983). For the affective aggressor, the intensity of emotions is heightened by a history of exposure to violent behavior or other personal victimization. She or he is engaged in a sustained struggle to manage high levels of confusion, anxiety, and anger resulting from past abuse or trauma. In that context, even minor stressors may push this person past his or her limits of emotional control.

Table 4.1
Patterns of Aggression

Pattern	Description
Overaroused Aggression	Unintentional, undirected aggression resulting from high energy and excessive arousal
Impulsive Aggression	Fight or flight response to an often mis-perceived precipitating event
Affective Aggression	Rageful aggression often rooted in past history of abuse and occurring as an exaggerated re-sponse to small offenses or incidents that are misperceived as menacing or hostile
Predatory Aggression	Overinterpretation of potential danger or in-sult leads to carefully planned efforts to reassert power or achieve reward perceived as denied by others
Instrumental Aggression	Aggression has, over time, become an internal-ized and primary means of maintaining per-sonal control and less directly represents the defensive response to perceived threat that is evident in the other patterns

Predatory aggression also occurs as a reaction to perceived (and often misperceived) environmental threat or wrongdoing, but differs from the impulsive and affective types in that the aggressive response to the precipi-tating event is planned or calculated rather than spontaneous. Finally, the instrumental pattern of aggression similarly arises from perceived vulnera-bility to others and lack of support. In contrast to some of the others, how-ever, the instrumental pattern of aggressive behavior becomes, over time, an internalized and primary means of maintaining personal control. It does not only represent the defensive response to an immediate perceived threat that is evident in the other patterns (Hunt, 1993).

The five common patterns of aggression described reveal evidence that the majority of aggression is a problem-solving or coping response that rep-resents a desperate though inefficient attempt on the part of the aggressive individual to maintain a balance of personal autonomy and influence in re-lationship to his or her environment. The specific ecology of violence as a coping response is most clearly visible among the impulsive, affective, and predatory patterns, where violence often occurs in a distinctive sequence or cycle of person-environment interactions. This sequential nature of violence has been identified by a number of investigators. It is commonly referred to in the literature as the "assault cycle" or the "cycle of violence" (Kaplan & Wheeler, 1983; Walker, Colvin, & Ramsey, 1995). We describe the cycle below.

THE CYCLE OF VIOLENCE

Those who have encountered acts of violence often state in bewilderment that the aggressor became violent without warning or provocation. However, the majority of violent episodes do not consist of a single, disruptive event, but instead involve a predictable chain of occurrences during which an individual attempts to maintain and subsequently to regain a sense of personal control in the face of rising anxiety and internal crisis. Given that most violent episodes seem to follow a predictable cycle, it is more likely that warning signals were present but not recognized and addressed by observers. Specific needs and symptoms of the violent individual, as well as corresponding environmental responses that are needed to appropriately address them, can be identified at each stage in a "cycle of violence." Within the cycle, it is the quality of the interaction or match between these individual and environmental variables at each stage that can determine whether a violent episode will accelerate or attenuate.

An understanding of the cycle of violence and the stage-specific ecology of a violent episode removes some of the mystery from the event and offers a framework for understanding, anticipating, and potentially affecting its course. Different prevention and intervention measures seem to be indicated for individuals who are at different stages in the cycle. For example, students who are at the beginning stages of the cycle often benefit from problem-solving techniques, whereas those at heightened stages tend to be incapable of problem solving and, instead, require firm and clear direction with regard to their immediate behavior. There is some variation in the way that different authors have labeled the distinct stages in the cycle of violence, but as a whole, we can glean a sequence of at least five interrelated events: triggering, escalation, crisis, recovery, and postcrisis depression. A synthesis of three models of the cycle of violence is presented in Table 4.2 (Kaplan & Wheeler, 1983; Treischman, Whittaker, & Brendtro, 1971; Walker, Colvin, & Ramsey, 1995).

Table 4.2
The Cycle of Aggression

Phase	Description	Response
Triggering	Effort to manage a vague, growing sense of discomfort, helplessness, or panic precipitate movement away from usual or baseline behavior patterns (e.g., anger, withdrawal, giddiness, etc.).	Help the person to identify or "package" the problem by talking about it.
Escalation	Failure of pesonal coping resources to offer relief leads to externalization of internal panic, usually in the form of overreaction to some minor stressor in the immediate environment.	Redirect toward activities that more appropriately afford a sense of self-control. Place support systems on alert.
Crisis	Aggressive behavior is employed in an effort to compensate for an increasing loss of self-control by exerting physical control over the immediate environment. Pointed violation of acceptable behavior limits may also represent a primitive plea for external intervention.	Utilize available support system to ensure safety and protect property. Discontinue packaging efforts in favor of firm, clear directives on what is needed to end the crisis.
Recovery	Fatigue or intervention lead to a progressive decline in crisis-stage symptoms and incremental movement toward a return of personal composure and control. Aggression is abated; hostility and opposition may still be evident.	Continue crisis-stage responses. Encourage any progress made toward crisis resolution. Desist from problem solving.
Post-crisis Depression	Physically and mentally exhausted, anger and opposition give way to interest in making reparations to victims, relieving guilt, and/or returning to normal activitiy.	Assist with reparations. Explore and identify aggression triggers, Identify nonaggressive responses to future triggers. Acknowledge progress made, work done.

Triggering

The cycle begins with an individual who is in the triggering stage. Here the person is struggling to manage a rising but as yet unspecified sense of anxiety or panic. The source of the distress may be either a real or imagined environmental threat or, in the case of affective aggression, generalized anxiety stemming from past victimization. Although symptoms can vary widely at this stage, a change in the individual's typical or baseline behavior (e.g., anger, withdrawal, giddiness) is usually apparent as a result of the burden of internal distress on his or her normal coping mechanisms. The professional at this point aims to help the person to identify and manage or, as Treicshman (1971) and his colleagues put it, "package the problem" by talking about it.

Escalation

If the person is unable to name and resolve the rising anxiety, the second, or escalation, stage may be entered, in which the inner anxiety is externalized through overreaction to some normally routine stressor. At this stage the individual attempts to compensate for an increasing loss of self-control by exerting greater control over the immediate environment through such means as threats, refusals, and verbal intimidation. Professional response at this stage involves a continuing effort to "package" the problem and to redirect the person toward activities that will more appropriately afford him or her a greater sense of self-control (e.g., assisting the counselor in a household task, writing down a list of concerns).

Crisis

The third or crisis stage is entered at the point that verbally or physically aggressive behaviors are emitted in the person's effort to manipulate the environment. Star (1984) and others (Treischman, Whittaker, & Brendtro, 1971) have suggested that the deliberate violation of behavioral limits seen at this stage may represent a primitive plea for external intervention, as well as a desperate effort to hold on to a sense of personal competence. At the crisis stage, a teacher or counselor replaces his or her efforts to understand and find solutions to the problem with actions to ensure safety and with firm, clear directives about what is expected and needed to end the crisis.

Recovery

Through intervention and/or physical fatigue, the individual at the crisis stage ultimately reaches the fourth stage, that of recovery, in which there is a progressive decline in the crisis stage symptoms and a gradual return of personal composure and control. The cessation of aggressive behavior at this stage does not necessarily mark the end of the cycle and a return to normal. Though no longer assaultive, the individual moving through the recovery stage process may continue to be angry, oppositional, and resistant to efforts to process the incident or to problem solve. Consequently, the helper response at this stage should include continuation of the crisis stage responses, coupled with encouragement for any progress made toward bringing an end to the crisis.

Postcrisis Depression

Postcrisis problem solving can effectively occur *only* after the individual has completed the recovery process and reached the final, or postcrisis depression, stage. At this point anger and opposition characteristically give way to remorse and self-reproach. Exhausted and often ashamed, the individual at this stage may be receptive to intervention efforts in an attempt to make reparations to victims, relieve guilt, and be able to return to normal activity (Kaplan & Wheeler, 1983). The useful helper response at this stage would be to encourage those activities and to identify alternatives to violence in future stressful situations.

APPLICATION: TAKING AN ECOLOGICAL APPROACH TO STUDENT VIOLENCE

Prevention and Intervention

An ecological perspective rests on an assumption that the personal and environmental variables in the equation for student violence are interrelated. Consequently, effective approaches to violence prevention and intervention will take into consideration the factors in both the student and in the educational environment that increase the potential for violent behavior to occur. To develop attentiveness to these multiple factors, educators need a guiding framework for understanding student violence within the larger context of each individual's environment. Kaplan and Wheeler (1983) have identified four key ecological variables in aggression that occur in human service settings: the individual student, the direct service provider (or in this case, the educator), the service setting, and the administrative environment (Figure 4.1). Effective violence prevention and intervention measures will be based upon an understanding of the reciprocal

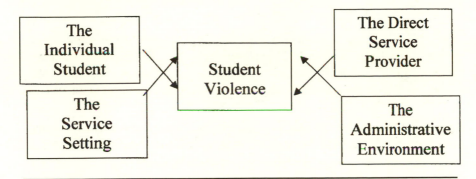

Figure 4.1
**Ecological Variables Related to Violence That Occurs within the Context of
a Human Services Setting**

relationships among the four variables. Specific considerations relevant to
each variable can be identified that have utility for educators in assessing
both the potential for student violence to occur and the level of individual
and/or organizational readiness for addressing its occurrence. These considerations are summarized below.

Factors in the Individual Student

History of Violence

History is the most powerful indicator of violent potential in an individual (Harris & Rice, 1997). In particular, past participation in violent behavior, exposure to family violence, and subjection to physical abuse all
warrant careful consideration as factors that may increase the possibility of
a student resorting to violent behavior in the face of stress. These factors
may also be useful in speculating about the specific pattern that future aggression will follow.

Substance Abuse

Though lacking in predictive value, evidence of alcohol or drug abuse
can be viewed as a predisposing factor for aggressive behavior in two ways:
Generally speaking, substance abuse may be symptomatic of the high levels
of stress and anxiety that foster aggression, and, in specific situations, it
may inhibit self-control and the choice of nonaggressive coping responses
to stressful events (Newhill, 1992). As such, a student's history of alcohol
and drug use should not be overlooked as a potential factor in the violence
equation, particularly when other predisposing factors are present.

Self-Control Problems

A student's recurrent need in the past for involuntary external assistance in dealing with personal problems (e.g., psychiatric, psychological, law enforcement) can indicate a problem with self-control and, consequently, an increased probability that out-of-control, aggressive behavior will occur in the future (Kaplan & Wheeler, 1983). Other signals of self-control problems include the student's boasting about losing control in the past or expressing fear of doing so in the future, and all such signals should be factored into an assessment of violence potential.

Demographic Factors

Assessment should also include consideration of social, political, cultural, and economic factors that may be acting generally to increase a student's sense of powerlessness and vulnerability and need for self-defensive action. For example, a teacher's failure to acknowledge issues of power related to racial or sexual oppression may create a climate of intimidation or insensitivity in the classroom, which could impact a student already at risk for violent behavior.

The Cycle of Violence

As discussed previously, any change in a student's primary or baseline mode of relating to others may be an indication of an impending and/or escalating cycle of violence. Attention to the moment within the cycle can alert counselors to the early warning signals of forthcoming violence. Such attention can also reduce the potential for further escalation, injury, and damage by eliminating the element of surprise and by providing a guide for stage-specific responses.

Factors in the Direct Service Provider

Views on Violence

Considerations regarding the service provider's level of readiness to confront student violence appropriately begin with an assessment of his or her views about violence and violent students (Kaplan & Wheeler, 1983). Effectiveness in working with potentially violent students may depend on the provider's ability to see violence as an ecological phenomenon and not as a problem that resides within the student (or any other single variable) alone. In the absence of such an ecological view, efforts toward either violence prevention or intervention are likely to be too narrow in scope to be effective. A provider's empathy for violent students stems partly from his or her ability to see violent behavior as the survival response depicted in the patterns and cycle of violence, and not merely as ungrounded hostility (Treischman, Whittaker, & Brendtro, 1971). Service providers who do not possess a working understanding of the patterns and the cycle of a violent episode may be more apt to view violent students with antipathy or fear. These are views that are clearly contrary to the establishment of a helping relationship, and, thus, are detrimental to the effectiveness of the educational process.

Self-Awareness

Helper self-awareness parallels understanding the nature of violence. Each is important for readying the helper deal with violent students. Direct service providers must assess the limits of their ability and willingness to deal with student violence and work within those limits. Specifically speaking, they must identify the aggressive student behaviors that are most likely to impair their professional effectiveness and be prepared to summon assistance when those behaviors are anticipated or encountered (Kaplan & Wheeler, 1983). Without thorough exploration of their own fears and capabilities, service providers run the risk of being oblivious or insensitive to the warning signals of impending student violence, as well as to opportunities for effective and safe intervention.

Demographic Factors

The variables of race, gender, ethnicity, and disability also impact expectations. They influence our definitions of normalcy. To successfully build an awareness of the influences of race, gender, ethnicity, and disability on violent behavior, direct service providers working with at-risk students must commit to critically examining their own personal values and biases regarding these issues. For example, as Sue and Sue suggest, if school staff members ascribe stereotypical traits to a racial minority or ethnic group, "It is reasonable to believe that they will behave differently toward the group and cause cognitive and behavioral changes among members of the group" (1990, p. 13). Providers need to develop a conscious awareness of how race, gender, ethnicity, and disability influence their own lives and the lives of students with whom they work (Gable, Bullock, & Harader, 1995). This ability to recognize differences and similarities among students can help service providers to challenge the too-common view of cultural difference as pathological or dangerous, and prevent misinterpretation and conflict in educator-student interactions, conflict that could elicit an aggressive episode.

Education/Training

Educators who expect to be effective in work with potentially violent students need to have prior training in the recognition of warning signals, the application of appropriate prevention and diffusion strategies, and the assurance of safety when prevention and diffusion measures fail (Kaplan & Wheeler, 1983; Star, 1984). As noted previously, those trained in the cycle of violence will be better prepared to identify specific student behaviors in a comprehensive context and to develop counseling strategies that are appropriate at all stages of the crisis. With prior training in the epidemiology of violence and the inherent limitations of the therapeutic process, educators are less likely to be caught off guard when student violence occurs or to view the occurrence of unanticipated violence as a personal failure (Brown, 1987). Because the frequency and magnitude of violent incidents continue to elude reliable prediction, educators in high-risk settings should have significant preparatory training in the use of support services. Specifically, they should be knowledgeable of all support resources available to their setting and have a clear understanding of the process for acquiring such resources whenever the conditions for violence exceed their own or the setting's assessed ability to ensure safety and student well-being.

Factors in the Service Setting

The makeup of the immediate setting for any educational activity warrants careful consideration in the development of violence prevention and intervention protocol. "Setting" here includes both general conditions and physical spaces. As a rule, the setting that is the least conducive to student violence is the one with qualities that maximize a student's feelings of safety and security and minimize sources of anxiety and frustration (Murdach, 1993). These important qualities are described below.

Clarity of Expectations

Foremost among the setting qualities that convey safety and reduce anxiety is the provision of well-defined parameters of expected and acceptable student behavior (Walker, Colvin, & Ramsey, 1995). Frustration and anxiety are reduced in a school setting by providing students with clearly articulated rules, procedural guidelines, and definitions of unacceptable behavior. Standing schedules, policies, and expectations should, whenever possible, be written and posted in view of those who are expected to follow them. These postings serve as "advance organizers," which prepare students for day-to-day expectations (Epanchin, Townsend, & Stoddard, 1994). For example, an initial advance organizer might involve a teacher telling students what the morning will be like, whereas a second advance organizer after lunch could be used to provide students with information regarding the structure of afternoon activities. When procedural and behavioral limits are clearly defined from the onset, students are afforded the security of knowing what is expected of them, and their need to test the limits of unacceptable behavior is reduced. Likewise reduced are the frustration and anxiety that result when unstated or ambiguous procedures are violated unintentionally.

Level of Restrictiveness

The student's knowledge that he or she maintains some control over decision-making processes that occur within the setting is related to a sense of "setting safety" (Kaplan & Wheeler, 1983). Consequently, limit-setting and directive-giving need not and, usually, should not, be done in an authoritarian manner. A very restrictive setting may exacerbate the feelings of personal threat and vulnerability that a student at risk for violent behavior is already likely to be experiencing (Newhill, 1992). The degree of restriction will vary, by necessity, according to the particular nature of a school.

One nonauthoritarian and effective means of setting norms is the "class meeting." It provides students with a forum for input into the development and enforcement of rules and expectations (Johns & Carr, 1995). In this approach, periodic meetings are scheduled in which the teacher presents rules and behavioral expectations to the class, leads an open discussion on the need for rules and on specific rules and their consequences, and modifies, adds, or deletes rules based on the discussion. Although some decisions on rules and expectations appropriately remain the responsibility of the teacher and the administration, class meetings enhance students' sense of personal competence and control by allowing them to voice their opinions and giving them an opportunity to be heard.

Physical Safety

The potential for violence is also influenced by the degree to which at-risk students feel physically safe within the setting. Qualities in the immediate service setting can, by either raising or lowering a student's sense of physical safety, enhance or reduce the potential for violence to occur (Walker, Colvin, & Ramsey, 1995). For example, a setting in which it is obvious that there is insufficient staffing to contain physical violence or that lacks an established and articulated plan for responding to violence may increase the anxiety of a student who fears losing self-control, becoming violent, and hurting self or others. In contrast, this student will have an increased sense of security, a reduction in anxiety, and, consequently, a decreased potential for violence in a setting where the presence of adequate crisis support is visible and clearly articulated.

Access to Exits

For the student who has escalated near the violent crisis stage, choosing to exit the immediate setting may sometimes be an appropriate alternative to injurious or damaging behavior as a means of reclaiming a sense of personal control (Kaplan & Wheeler, 1983). Arranging settings to provide students with clear and unobstructed access to exits may facilitate their choice of self-removal, over personal assault or property damage, as a coping response to session intensity. This arrangement may also reduce the risk and extent of injury or damage in the event of a violent episode by creating a path of least resistance between the violent student and relief from the immediate source of his or her distress. School personnel should carefully evaluate the means by which potentially violent students might independently remove themselves to avoid an outburst. For example, some classes might have an established "time out" area within the classroom, whereas others might have a predetermined, supervised area for time out away from the classroom such as the counselor's or principal's office. If self-removal is not an acceptable option for violent students, a clear plan as to how their behavior will be safely contained is all the more important.

Access to Weapons

School settings should routinely be arranged to minimize the availability of potential weapons to students (Walker, Colvin, & Ramsey, 1995). For example, unnecessary items that frequently serve as weapons such as letter openers, message skewers, heavy paperweights, and so on should be eliminated from the classroom. Potential weapons necessary for instruction such as dissecting tools, burners, and sharp compasses should be kept inaccessible to students except when they are in classroom use. Weapons obviously increase both the risk and potential severity of injury and damage during a violent episode. In addition, they increase the very likelihood of violence. The presence of potential weapons is "tempting," in that it may empower at-risk individuals to choose aggression, rather than self-removal, as a means to personal control and emotional relief. Though it is impossible to eliminate student access to weapons completely, it is important that their access by potentially violent students be minimized to the greatest extent possible.

The Administrative Environment

Guiding Philosophy, Policy, and Procedure

It is the responsibility of any school's administration to acknowledge serious student crises as an inherent hazard of the services they provide. Administrators should avoid the tendency to fault an individual service provider (e.g., teacher or counselor) when such crises occur (Brown, 1987). Only with ownership of responsibility for student violence prevention and intervention at the administration level will there likely be the shift from individual blame to the development of policies and procedures that address the comprehensive, ecological antecedents of the problem. Such ownership can espoused in an administration-wide recognition of the difficulties inherent in predicting and preventing violence and in providing active support for those who provide direct services to students who become violent. This ownership of shared responsibility for preventing aggression is operationalized through specific policies and procedures that provide all staff at all levels with the formal training, supervision, and professional collaboration opportunities that they need to effectively and safely implement violence prevention and intervention initiatives. The relevance of these opportunities is described below.

Training Opportunities

As noted previously, the incidence, intensity, and impact of student violence all appear to be lessened when there has been adequate prior preparation for the crisis. The degree to which regular opportunities for formal training in violence prevention and intervention are made available to school personnel may reflect the level of importance and priority being afforded to the crisis of student violence by the educational administration. Demonstrated support from the leadership for the standardized training of all staff in topics such as violence epidemiology, prevention, and intervention is a strong indication of ownership of the problem of student violence at an administrative level.

Opportunities for Supervisory Guidance and Support

Training alone is insufficient preparation for coping with the actual experience of student violence (McAdams & Foster, 1999). Those school personnel who are providing direct services to youth who are at risk for violent behavior require ongoing individual and/or group supervision around both potential and real experiences with student violence. Such supervision is necessary to address the inevitable gap between theory (acquired in training) and professional practice, and it should be consistent with school philosophy, policy, and procedure. Given that the persistent stress of violence in the school setting may be one cause of burnout, the school-based supervisor would employ strategies to assist and support the supervisee in both preparing for and processing violent student crises. With appropriate supervisory support to ensure positive learning from the event, some counselors who have encountered violence have reported that the crisis ultimately contributed to their professional growth as clinicians. They have also indicated that the negative psychological impact of violence seems to be lessened when a counselor or other service provider has had ongoing individual supervision (McAdams & Foster, 1999).

Opportunities for Ongoing Interprofessional Collaboration

An attitude of schoolwide ownership of student violence prevention and intervention is conveyed by the existence of formal provisions for collaboration among staff at all levels in the design and delivery of services to students who are at risk for crisis behavior (Brown, 1987; Kaplan & Wheeler, 1983). One such provision involves the development of standardized procedures to promote the sharing of expertise and information among the various academic and support personnel assigned to work with at-risk student cases such as the special education teachers, school counselors, and school psychologists. Establishing a protocol such as a "team meeting" for both routine and spontaneous review of such cases by all involved staff represents an administration's shared concern for student violence issues. Another form of administrative support involves the creation and documentation of formal procedures for summoning immediate, physical assistance from colleagues when staff are contending with threatening or violent student episodes (e.g., a teacher pounding on the classroom wall as a known signal). The standardization of such procedures demonstrates recognition by the administration that student violence is an inherent risk of its service rather than a rare exception. A final provision of support involves the creation of formal arrangements with other community services (e.g., mental health, law enforcement, medical) for assistance in dealing with violent students. The formalization of arrangements for community assistance gives evidence of administrative support for the ecological view that violent students cannot be adequately served in isolation from their community environment.

CONCLUSION

The work of the professional educator can be both deeply satisfying and disturbing. The disturbance can be compounded when the educator tries to work with seriously disturbed students. Helping students with their academic progress can become confounded by many personal and emotional factors that are beyond the scope of an educational program. Schools are faced with increasing numbers of students who have diverse and complex problems, including violent behavior. For beginning educators, the failure to anticipate and prevent serious student violence is likely to be viewed as both a personal failure and a reason for serious and often disabling professional self-doubt. At the same time, however, that encounter can be a stimulus for continued personal and professional growth. Such development can occur when education/training programs and supervision are available to provide adequate preparation prior to a violent event, as well as once it has occurred. Incorporating an ecological framework in conceptualizing student violence appropriately shifts the complete locus and blame away from individual students or staff members. The ecological framework can lead to safer and more effective prevention and intervention efforts, ones that appropriately take into account the multiple causes of the problem.

REFERENCES

Brown, H.N. (1987). The impact of suicide on psychiatrists in training. *Comprehensive Psychiatry, 28,* 101–112.

Epanchin, B.C., Townsend, B., & Stoddard, K. (1994). *Constructive classroom management.* Pacific Grove, CA: Brooks/Cole Publishing Company.

Gable, R.A., Bullock, L.M., & Harader, D.L. (1995). Schools in transition: The challenge of clients with aggressive and violent behavior. *Preventing School Failure, 39,* 29–34.

Harris, G.T., & Rice, M.E. (1997). Risk appraisal and management of violent behavior. *Psychiatric Services, 48* (9), 1168–1176.

Hunt, R. (1993). Neurological patterns of aggression. *Journal of Emotional and Behavioral Problems, 2* (1), 14–20.

Johns, J.H., & Carr, V.G. (1995). *Techniques for managing verbally and physically aggressive students.* Denver: Love Publishing Company.

Kaplan. S.G., & Wheeler, E.G. (1983). Survival skills for working with potentially violent clients. *Journal of Contemporary Social Work, 64,* 339–346.

Kazdin, A. (1993). Treatment of conduct disorder: Progress and directions in psychotherapy research. *Development and Psychology, 5* (1/2), 277–310.

McAdams, C.R., & Foster, V.A. (1999). A conceptual framework for understanding client violence in residential treatment. *Child and Youth Care Forum, 28* (5), 307–328.

Monahan, J. (1984). The prediction of violent behavior: Toward a second generation of theory and policy. *American Journal of Psychiatry, 141* (1), 10–15.

Murdach, A.D. (1993). Working with potentially assaultive clients. *Health & Social Work, 18* (4), 307–312.

Newhill, C. (1992). Assessing danger to others in clinical social work practice. *Social Service Review, 66,* 64–84.

Star, B. (1984). Patient violence/therapist safety. *Social Work, 29,* 225–230.

Sue, D.W., & Sue, S. (1990). *Counseling the culturally different: Theory and practice.* New York: Wiley.

Treischman, A.E., Whittaker, J.K., & Brendtro, L.K. (1971). *The other 23 hours.* Hawthorne, NY: Aldine de Gruyter.

Walker, H.M., Colvin, G., & Ramsey, E. (1995). *Antisocial behavior in school: Strategies and best practices.* Pacific Grove, CA: Prentice-Hall.

5

Creating Home–School Connections: Opportunities and Barriers

Denyse Dorries

Research in child development suggests that the single most important influence on a child's development is the family and the second most important environmental influence is the school (Epstein, 1992; Valentine, 1992). When these resources are combined, their influence is maximized. Children whose parents are connected to the school in positive ways have distinct advantages, both academically and behaviorally (Christenson & Conoley, 1992; Comer & Haynes, 1991; Epstein 1986, 1995; Hoover-Dempsey & Sandler, 1995). Increases in academic performance, higher test scores, improved student self-esteem, better attitudes toward school, improved attendance, and a reduction of inappropriate behaviors are all correlated with parent involvement (Christenson, Rounds, & Franklin, 1992; Epstein, 1986, 1992, 1995).

When such a relationship exists, the effects are two-way: Parents report that they implement teacher recommendations for assisting their children at home, and teachers report feeling more positively toward children in schools (Epstein, 1986). The effects of school practices on parent involvement are clear. Schools that actively promote positive interactions with families can dramatically influence the way that those families interact with the schools, as well as with their children. More important, when schools make a conscious effort to solicit parents' help in fostering children's learning, student achievement increases and consequently inappro-priate behaviors decrease (Arroyo, Gable, & Selig, this volume; Clark, this volume; Epstein, 1992).

HOME-SCHOOL LINKAGES: THE PROBLEMS AND THE POSSIBILITIES

Almost all parents and guardians care about their children in a funda-mental way. They want them to succeed. Most want information from the schools to be better able to help their children learn (Epstein, 1995). Eighty percent to 90 percent of parents of school-age children report that they believe the school should tell them how to help their child (Epstein, 1992). Similarly, almost all teachers and administrators would like to in-volve families, but many do not know how to go about building positive connections (Epstein, 1995). Overall trends in home-school interaction suggest that there is evidence that significant problems exist in this area and need to be addressed. There is hope, however. The following trends in the literature illustrate the powerful role that school staff can play in over-coming barriers to home-school linkages:

- As might be expected, affluent communities have more positive family in-volvement unless the school personnel in economically distressed communi-ties are invested in building positive partnerships with their students' families (Caldas & Bankston, 1999; Epstein et al., 1997).

- Single parents, working parents, parents who live at a distance from the school, and fathers are less involved at the school building, unless the school organizes opportunities for involvement of these participants at different times and loca-tions (Epstein et al., 1997).

- School staff in economically deprived areas have a tendency to make more fre-quent contacts with families about problems that children are having than about successes, unless they make an intentional effort to contact parents about positive accomplishments of their students (Epstein et al., 1997).

- Parent involvement tends to decline across the grades unless schools and teach-ers are committed to implementing practices that facilitate home-school part-nerships (Epstein et al., 1997; McCarthey, 2000).

The effect of school practices on parent involvement is clear. Schools that foster positive interactions with families dramatically influence the way that those families interact with the schools, as well as with their chil-dren. When schools make a conscious effort to solicit parents' help in fos-tering children's learning, student achievement increases (Epstein, 1992).

Further, positive home-school relationships help establish the ecological context necessary for prevention of violence (McAdams & Foster, this volume). Therefore, it is important to examine what we know about factors that impede and those that facilitate positive home-school involvement.

BARRIERS TO POSITIVE HOME-SCHOOL CONNECTIONS

There are both school factors and home factors that interfere with the creation of positive home-school connections. Many roadblocks exist that steer schools away from reaching out to families and cause friction between home and school.

School Factors

The School Effectiveness Movement

Home-school connections have declined since the emergence of the school effectiveness or "high-stakes testing" movement (Caldas & Bankston, 1999). This movement has discounted the centrality of family involvement as a determiner of student outcomes by emphasizing almost exclusively the role of school staff's expectancies and practices in addressing student achievement (Caldas & Bankston, 1999). Despite the data indicating that students from single parent homes are at a distinct academic disadvantage and perform more poorly on academic measures, the schools are effectively ignoring the impact of the home in the equation of student educational achievement (Caldas & Bankston, 1999). When schools ignore family involvement, they neglect a powerful resource.

Expecting Students to Make the Connections

Educators' assumptions that students can make home-school connections on their own pose another barrier to effective home-school connections. This belief is more congruent with a middle-class view that students and families do not need help in making connections (Hoover-Dempsey & Sandler, 1995). Almost all students want their families to be involved in their schools but many require additional direction from the teachers on how to make this possible (Epstein et al., 1997). Schools need to consider ways to help the students engage their families around school-related learning activities.

Teachers' Views of Parents' Roles

Misperceptions on the part of school personnel about appropriate parent-teacher roles can interfere with home-school interactions. Teachers may perceive parents as being incapable or incompetent to assist their students with the schoolwork (McCarthey, 2000). Teachers might also consider parent involvement as intrusive, particularly when teachers' time is so limited that they may feel it is a waste of their time to focus on individual families. There is a significant difference between teachers who view education as a shared responsibility and those who believe that only the teacher can create an optimal learning environment.

Discontinuity

Disparities between home and school in such areas as values, communication patterns, expectations, and discipline can create friction (Watkins, 1997). For example, differences in use of touch, proximity control, and unspoken rules for eye contact can cause misunderstanding and confusion in both students and teachers (Swap, 1992). Other differences with regard to teaching styles and learning may be subtler but can result in academic problems if teachers ignore their implications.

Administrators' Roles

The attitudes and behaviors of administrators can be a barrier to home-school connections. Administrators can set the tone in promoting a positive school climate, one that welcomes parents (Clark, this volume). However, some administrators may discourage parents through a lack of awareness of variables that influence parent involvement. For example, meetings with parents may be too formal. Often too much jargon may be used that confuses and intimidates parents (Watkins, 1997). Also, adherence to one worldview about "normal" or about "standards" on the part of school personnel might deter positive interactions, as in the case of schools and school staff who do not value cultural diversity and appreciate individual differences. Such schools might ignore the experiences of families of children with disabilities. By ignoring this difference, the school in essence invalidates the family's perspective, which can result in hostility and misunderstandings. Administrators must intentionally decide to create schools that are inviting to parents, not only to increase student learning but also to produce an environment that prevents violence (McAdams & Foster, this volume).

Family Factors

Schools are not the only system that can impede the development of productive home-school connections; there are also factors in families that interfere with the process.

Prior Experiences

Education has become so complex in the past decade that many family members, who may have had a negative experience in school themselves, retain into adulthood a sense of inadequacy with regard to dealing with schools. Because of these preconceived images, they may become defensive when schools attempt to connect with them (Epstein, 1995; McCarthey, 2000).

Privacy Issues

Many parents, especially those from minority and low socioeconomic status (SES) groups, may value keeping home and school separate because they do not want school personnel encroaching on their home or discounting their perspectives. No matter how inviting the school atmosphere, some families, because of either their own or their child's past experiences with school, are still suspicious of the school staff's intentions and do not accept the invitation to interact. These families may not want to risk having another bad experience with school personnel.

Overcommitted Lives

Not only has education become more complex but also family life has become more complicated in our era. The day-to-day demands of being a parent and a partner and of having a job can impose too many impediments to the making of home-school connections. Single parents and dual earners often cannot and do not participate at the school building level (Epstein, 1986). Parents who work often do not have the time or resources to visit the schools on a regular basis. However, studies have demonstrated that although parents from such families may not be physically present in the school building, they are just as likely as more affluent, single-earner families to help their children with schoolwork (Epstein, 1992).

Confidence

Some parents may have a lack of self-efficacy, or confidence, in some areas of parenting. Consequently, they are reluctant to receive any negative feedback from school personnel. Although the majority of parents try to help their children at home, many do not know if they are doing the right things (Epstein et al., 1997). For example, parents are often confused about how much help they should give their children with regard to homework. Parents who question their ability to assist their child may avoid interactions that would place them in a position to be criticized by school personnel (Epstein et al., 1997).

Logistics

Finally, families may want to connect and share ideas with school personnel but do not know how to go about this process (McCarthey, 2000). Family schedules may preclude their coming to the school building during regular school hours, and they may be reluctant to call a teacher at night.

ON THE POSITIVE SIDE: SCHOOL VARIABLES THAT FACILITATE HOME-SCHOOL CONNECTIONS

Given the aforementioned barriers, creating home-school linkages seems daunting. However, there is evidence that, with initiative and conscious intent, schools can include families more fully in the work of education. Research suggests that all forms of parental involvement strategies are useful; however, programs that are well planned, comprehensive, and enduring and that offer more options for parents to be involved with their children are the most effective (Christenson, Rounds, & Franklin, 1992; Epstein et al., 1997). It is not enough to invite parents to come into the schools. Parents need to become an integral part of the instructional program.

Essential Preconditions

Before any specific methods are implemented, three preconditions should be present. These conditions might ensure the success of the home-school linkage effort. They are attitudes and practices about empowerment, communication, and staff training.

Having an Empowerment and Competency Focus

In order to establish the context in which parents will allow teachers to coach them in home instruction, the connection between the home and school must be built on respect and mutual trust. Student learning should be viewed as a shared responsibility. Teachers must take a competency-based approach that helps to empower parents by emphasizing the importance of the role of the parent in improving student learning and behavior. When school personnel accentuate the importance of parents' roles in improving student learning and behavior, parents are more likely to participate in helping their children with learning (Watkins, 1997). Empowered parents are more likely to want to know how to supplement their child's learning and are more open to receive teacher instruction in this area (Epstein et al., 1997). When parents' strengths are emphasized, they become more responsive to the school's leadership in instructional issues.

Emphasizing Two-Way Communication

Another path for establishing the preconditions necessary for positive home reinforcement of student learning is two-way communication. In order for the relationship between the parents and school to be based on mutual respect and shared responsibility, communication must flow in both directions. Parents need to be made aware of the nature of the curriculum, school policies (e.g., grading procedures) and specific classroom rules (e.g., will late work be accepted?). However, school personnel need to become familiar with parents' priorities, a child's background, and the different ways that parents currently attempt to enhance their child's learning. Based on this shared knowledge, teachers can then provide information about how the family can best supplement the child's learning and do it in a way that is respectful of the family's time, values, and current practices (Epstein, 1992). For example, if a child comes from a single parent home, he or she may need modifications to their homework or additional afterschool assistance depending on the work schedule of the parent.

Providing Training for School Staff in Home-School Linkages

In-service staff development, as well as preservice training, need to be provided for teachers and administrators. Teachers traditionally receive the least amount of preservice training in the area of effective strategies for working with parents (Caldas & Bankston, 1999). This training addresses interaction patterns and communication skills needed to foster positive expectations and partnerships with parents. It is needed to ensure that there are more than just a small core of caring teachers and administrators who are willing to reach out to the families (Epstein et al., 1997). Every teacher should be expected to reach out to families because it will, in the long run, benefit the students in multiple ways.

In sum, it is the school's job to create the conditions that encourage families to be more directly involved in their children's education.

SPECIFIC STRATEGIES FOR FOSTERING
HOME-SCHOOL LINKAGES

Promising Methods

Two of the most promising methods of linking families and schools are encouraging complementary home instruction and maximizing methods for communication between all parties. These two strategies are described here.

Encouraging Home Instruction

Parental involvement in home instruction is one of the most effective ways to improve children's learning and motivation (Watkins, 1997). It is also the most underutilized strategy (Watkins, 1997). An outreach program that aims at teaching parents how to do home instruction must become a part of each school's standard operating procedures.

The quality of the interactions between the parent and child around learning issues correlates highly with student outcomes (McCarthey, 2000). Families know that providing learning assistance at home is important, but most need to learn strategies for enhancing learning at home (Hoover-Dempsey & Sandler, 1995).

Thus, in addition to the positive home-school connections, specific school programs must be designed to increase the interaction between the child and parent around instruction (Epstein, 1986). Parents need to receive clear directions as to how to assist their child and may need opportunities to examine and create curriculum materials and/or model teacher strategies (Watkins, 1997). Opportunities to interact and communicate with teachers must be created and facilitated by the school.

One method for promoting home instruction is to provide parents with opportunities to learn together with their children in an environment that is inviting and nonthreatening. The schools can invite parents and their children to parent-teacher conferences that are held frequently at various times and locations, such as at local churches or in local community centers. Parents often need encouragement to create or find materials that they can use at home with their children. The school might provide back-to-school nights and/or weekend enrichment courses for parents with "make-it-take-it" activities. For example, teachers can give parents the vocabulary words that will be dealt with in the next few reading assignments and have the parents create games and flash cards that the parents can take home at the end of the workshop. The children can also participate in such an activity which can further enhances their learning through fun activities. Workshops might have specific themes devoted to content areas (math, reading, science, and social studies) in order to enhance the learning in a particular area.

The schools need to offer frequent opportunities for joint learning activities for students and their families. An effective strategy that involves the whole family in the student's learning is for the teacher to assign "family writing conference," where the student records family stories and brings them to school to share. Teachers can provide interactive homework designed for students to talk to adults in their home, or a "hands-on" experience with computers in which parents and students learn skills together. These activities can reinforce student skills while teaching new ways of doing research or word processing. This strategy also gives the teacher a richer, more complex understanding of the students' life.

One of the most confusing issues for parents is their role in daily homework. Parents need to be provided specific guidance concerning when and how to assist with homework. Many parents are unclear with regard to how much and in what ways they should supervise homework; for example, should they correct homework? Homework hotlines have been found to be beneficial for everyone involved because it can verify homework assignments and/or assist callers with their assignments (Fuller & Olsen, 1998).

Summer is a time in which many children backslide with regard to academic skills. Teachers might want to create summer home learning packets with explicit instructions in order to encourage continued learning and reinforcement through the vacation time.

Establishing Vehicles for Communication

There is no one correct way to communicate with parents. Communications can take a number of different forms. Class newsletters, e-mail, Web sites, faxes, and computerized phone messages can give parents specific daily or weekly information and provide a better connection for parents to the school. For example, Scaringello (this volume) has laid out a model for using computers to foster communication between parents and schools. Flyers, letters, and home pages must clearly explain the ways in which parents can become a part of the child's education.

The timing of communications is also very important. Communication needs to be established early in the school year, before problems occur and then become ongoing. Parents need to informed of problems well before report card time and informed of the good things that are happening at school as well (Baker, 1997). For example, often teachers of children with special needs develop a home-school journal, a form of two-way communication. Such a journal is helpful in maintaining day-to-day communication that addresses areas of concern (Fuller & Olsen, 1998). Teachers, parents, and students can all contribute to the journal.

However, the ways in which schools reach out to parents, the time of day for the conferences, assemblies, and workshops, as well as the location of these events, speaks more loudly than the flyer that carries the information home to them (Griffith, 1998). In order to communicate effectively with parents, schools need to schedule conferences, workshops, and activities for the convenience of those parents who are the least likely to be able to attend due to work, distance, or child care needs.

CONCLUSION

Enhancing home-school connections requires the intention by school staff to reach out to families in positive ways. Schools need to have a well-trained staff who possess strong communication and problem-solving skills and are committed to creating opportunities for all parents to participate in their child's education. Joining the forces of schools and families increases the likelihood that students will succeed in learning both the academic and social skills necessary for a productive life. Strong positive partnerships between the home and school promote students' learning and provide the environment that fosters improved psychosocial adjustment in students.

REFERENCES

Baker, A. (1997). Improving parent involvement programs and practice: A qualitative study of parent perceptions. *School Community Journal, 7* (1), 9–34.

Caldas, S., & Bankston, C.L. (1999). Multilevel examination of student, school, and district-level effects on academic achievement. *Journal of Educational Research, 93* (2), 91–100.

Christenson, S.L., & Conoley, J.C. (1992). *Home-school collaboration: Enhancing children's academic and social competence.* Silver Spring, MD: National Association of School Psychologists.

Christenson, S.L., Rounds, T., & Franklin, M.J. (1992). Home-school collaboration: Effects, issues, and opportunities. In S.L. Christenson & J.C. Conoley (Eds.), *Home-school collaboration: Enhancing children's academic and social competence* (pp. 19–51). Washington, DC: National Association of School Psychologists.

Comer, J.P., & Haynes, N.M. (1991). Parent involvement in schools: An ecological approach. *Elementary School Journal, 91,* 271–277.

Epstein, J. (1986). Parent's reactions to teacher practices of parent involvement. *The Elementary School Journal*, 86, 277–294.

Epstein, J. (1995). School/family/community/ partnerships. *Phi Delta Kappan*, 5, 701–712.

Epstein, J., Coates, L., Salinas, K.C., Sanders, M.G., & Simon, B.S. (1997). *School, family, and community partnerships*. Thousand Oaks, CA: Corwin Press.

Epstein, J.L. (1992). School and family partnerships: Leadership roles for school psychologists. In S.L. Christenson & J.C. Conoley (Eds.), *Home-school collaboration: Enhancing children's academic and social competence* (pp. 499–515). Silver Spring, MD: National Association of School Psychologists.

Fuller, M.L., & Olsen, G. (1998). *Home-school relations*. Neeham Heights, MA: Allyn & Bacon.

Griffith, J. (1998). The relation of school structure and social environment to parent involvement in elementary schools. *Elementary School Journal*, 99 (1), 53–78.

Hoover-Dempsey, K.V., & Sandler, H.M. (1995). Parental involvement in children's education: Why does it make a difference? *Teachers College Record*, 95, 310–331.

McCarthey, S.J. (2000). Home-school connections: A review of the literature. *Journal of Educational Research*, 93 (3), 145–153.

Swap, S.M. (1992). Parent involvement and success for all children: What we know now. In S.L. Christenson & J.C. Conoley (Eds.), *Home-school collaboration: Enhancing children's academic and social competence* (pp. 53–80). Silver Spring, MD: National Association of School Psychologists.

Valentine, M.R. (1992). How to deal with difficult school discipline problems: A family systems approach adapted for schools. In S.L. Christenson & J.C. Conoley (Eds.), *Home-school collaboration: Enhancing children's academic and social competence* (pp. 357–382). Silver Spring, MD: National Association of School Psychologists.

Watkins, T.J. (1997). Teacher communications, child achievement, and parent traits in parent involvement models. *Journal of Educational Research*, 91 (1), 3–13.

6

Using Multiple Perspectives to Construct Schools for Troubled Youth

Lynn Doyle

What do we mean by the term "troubled youth"? Clear definitions elude us, but all educators recognize who their troubled students are. They are students who may be called violent, aggressive, withdrawn, bullied, depressed, anorexic, poor, or, simply, "at-risk." They are the ones who exhibit psychological and social problems and cause us concern beyond academics; in fact, some of them may be academically successful. What they have in common is that they are in distress, and too many of their schools do not see their difficulty as the school's responsibility.

Just as each individual sees the world in different ways, schools also have ways of "seeing." The educators in each school collectively make choices about how they view the role of their school in relation to troubled youth. Leaders in the school influence these views. These leaders can be teachers, parents, and community representatives, but they typically are the school administrators. The purpose of this chapter is to present a "multiple-perspectives" framework for critiquing current and alternative school practices for troubled youth. Readers can additionally use this framework as a point of departure for planning in their own settings.

THREE PERSPECTIVES

Education is a field that borrows from many disciplines. Thus, educational theorists have discussed taking multiple perspectives in education from foundations that range from philosophy to psychology to sociology. For example, some theorists have drawn upon the work of the philosopher Jurgen Habermas (e.g., Habermas, 1979) to propose that "disorienting dilemmas" can help alter routines and precipitate change. Others have looked to cognitive stage theories in adult development to describe leadership and teaching practices (e.g., Kegan & Lahey, 1984).

Another foundation that has been used widely in the discussion of multiple perspectives emerges from the work of Burrell and Morgan (1979). Based on their work, three general paradigms have been used to describe how schools are led and organized. They are the functionalist, the constructivist, and the critical (for further discussion, see Capper, 1993; Denzin, 1994; Doyle, 1995; Foster, 1989; Reitzug, 1994a; Sirotnik & Oakes, 1986; Skrtic, 1991; and Slater, 1995). These three constitute the framework for this chapter.

The Functionalist Perspective

Functionalism is a general outlook in which practicality and utility are stressed, rather than process and meaning. According to the functionalist perspective, knowledge and learning are products of rationality and objectivity. Burrell and Morgan describe functionalism thus: "[It is] firmly rooted in the sociology of regulation and approaches its subject matter from an objectivist point of view.... It is characterised by a concern for providing explanations of the status quo, social order, consensus, social integration, solidarity, need satisfaction and actuality. It approaches these general sociological concerns from a standpoint which tends to be realist, positivist, determinist and nomothetic [i.e., law seeking]" (1979, pp. 25–26). Examples of several educational practices that have emerged from the functionalist perspective include programmed instruction, standardized testing, and the categorization of students through legislation and funding mechanisms.

The Constructivist Perspective

Another way to examine schools is through a constructivist lens. Constructivism is the view that emphasizes emerging social processes rather than regulation and order. McAuliffe and Lovell (2000) point out that the constructivist perspective also shares much with postmodernist philosophy in that constructivists view meanings as subjective and socially created by people's perceptions. For example, those holding a more functionalist point of view contend that knowledge exists and that researchers reveal this knowledge base. They argue that students learn this body of existing knowledge through discrete units, which are transmitted and mastered in a specific linear progression. Constructivists, on the other hand, purport that knowledge does not objectively exist but is created by the interrelationships of people with each other and their environments. Because knowledge is socially constructed, learning is therefore a social act. For educational practitioners then, it follows that teachers should make learning social through such strategies as cooperative learning and participatory decision making. From these teaching strategies, it also follows that student assessment would include collaborative evaluation methods, such as peer-reviewed demonstrations and performances.

The Critical Perspective

Theorists holding a critically oriented perspective attend especially to power. They encourage the study of social oppression and promote social advocacy (Aronowitz & Giroux, 1991; Freire, 1970). Several philosophical foundations that fall under the critical perspective include critical feminism, queer theory, critical theory, and neomarxism. A critical view differs most from functionalism and constructivism in its clear ideological agenda to emancipate oppressed persons from the control of those holding power over them. Through a critical lens, educators view their schools as communities of learners rather than "cults of efficiency" (Callahan, 1962). Critical educators reconsider the functionalist thinking that undergirds practices in most schools of today and commit to larger issues of social justice. For example, when asked, "Why do we in education provide food programs for students in our schools?" most educators might respond, "If students are hungry, they cannot learn as well." A critical perspective would encourage us to answer, "We feed students because it is morally and ethically right to feed hungry people." The emphasis shifts from a marketable product to a moral, ethical, and caring process.

The way that schools deal with home-school conferences provides an example of the critical perspective in practice. A critical school would invite empowered parents or guardians to meet, collaborate, and to share expertise with school staff members in order to develop educational plans for their children. This process stands in strong contrast to current practices, in which teachers as experts transmit summaries of student successes or failures to nonparticipative, powerless guardians.

HOW SCHOOLS VIEW TROUBLED YOUTH: A CALL FOR MULTIPLE PERSPECTIVES

Although the three perspectives, that is, functionalist, constructivist, and critical, appear to be mutually exclusive, in practice they do not have to be. Each, as a partial understanding, can contribute to the way that schools provide services to troubled youth. Functionalism has been and continues to be the dominant perspective in most schools. In many ways functionalist thought has served education well. Through this perspective educators have developed measurement instruments, accountability systems, computer monitoring tools, and laws that mandate equal access. But have we gone too far? Is there an overemphasis on regulation that harms the individuals whom these advances purport to serve? Does the functionalist perspective address the needs of all students, particularly those in need of specialized and individualized care, or has it lost track of its purposes in favor of efficiency, order, and blindly preserving a status quo? In their book, *Meeting the Needs of Students of ALL Abilities*, Capper, Frattura, and Keyes (2000) point out several ironies in schools that can result from narrow functionalist thinking. They consider the case of a sixteen-year-old student who commits a severe crime while attending school. If found guilty and incarcerated, this student, by law, must receive an education while she or he is in jail because the Compulsory Education Act mandates it. However, if she or he is not incarcerated, the school can legally deny this student (and many others) an education through expulsion and suspension. It is ironic that, although prisons cannot deny students an education, public schools, the very heart of education in this country, can.

A school's use of these three perspectives ideally lies along a continuum and incorporates multiple perspectives. Situations in which one perspective would be used exclusively are rare, but possible. For example, in the case of a school violence incident, one perspective is likely to be primary during the emergency. The school might need a few leaders to be as functionalist as possible in removing all staff and students from the building quickly and efficiently. However, the aftermath of a violent incident poses a far different situation, one that requires the use of multiple perspectives to deal with students' psychological and social needs. In order to heal and to prevent future incidents, we need to consider the recommendations of McAuliffe, who asserts in the preface of this volume that schools need to "widen the circle of community for all youth." Educators need to widen the circle by considering not only the needs of the victims and witnesses of these events, but also those of the perpetrators. Exclusive use of the functionalist perspective blames and punishes. Such an approach appears to provide the closure that the community so desperately seeks; however, these complex human events defy such closure. Educators instead need to "look for trouble" before these events occur and use multiple perspectives as they seek preventive solutions. It takes considerable effort and reflective practice to widen the circle in which we are comfortable. The purpose of this chapter is to encourage such effort and reflection, to invite readers to dance with the three partners of functionalism, constructivism, and critical theory.

In this chapter I use these three perspectives to discuss the four domains of schools as defined by Rowan (1995): teaching, leadership, organization, and context (see Table 6.1 for a summary of the framework). I then discuss how schools might view troubled youth using a multiple perspective approach. Readers can use this framework to reflect on and integrate the various chapters in this volume. They might also use this framework to analyze beliefs and practices in their own environments and plot new directions.

Teaching

Teaching is the first of Rowan's (1995) four domains. Teaching that emerges from a functionalist perspective transmits a product to learners. That product is a specified curriculum composed of discrete and linear units. Delivery of the product is typically measured through objective, standardized tests. Functionalist teaching fosters the idea that "one size fits all." Examples of functionalist teaching include standards of learning and a rigid curriculum delivered through programmed instruction and pacing guides. Although prevalent in many schools, functionalist teaching does not accommodate differences and the uniqueness of each student.

In contrast, constructivist teaching is process oriented. Its purpose is to transform learners into critical thinkers and collaborative problem solvers. Constructivist teachers recognize the individual differences within their students and see these differences as contributions to the collective rather than deviance as a functionalist view would. Constructivist teaching stresses the interrelatedness of learning through team teaching and hands-on instruction. Teaching moves from functionalist methods that emphasize sequenced mastery of basic skills to methods that build schemata or cognitive structures. Students learn by organizing knowledge into cognitive structures such as cognitive schema, frames, and scripts. These cognitive structures serve as maps and frameworks to help students organize, reorganize, and combine information with their prior knowledge. The students' levels of prior knowledge and mapping abilities differentiate them into groups of experts and novices. In cooperative learning groups,

Table 6.1
A Contrast of Perspectives for Schools

	Functionalist	Constructivist	Critical
Teaching	Transmits curriculum	Transforms learners	Develops learners as social advocates
	Emphasis on established knowledge base	Emphasis on cognitive struc-tures	Emphasis on an ideology of inclusion and redistribution of power
	Product oriented	Process oriented	Process oriented
Leadership	Autocratic	Collaborative	Socially reformative
	Principal at apex of a hierarchy	Principal at center of the organization	Principal empowers groups that are disenfran-chised
	Assigned power through positions	Shared power	Redistribution and exchange of power
Organization	Hierarchical	Collaborative	Reformative
	Bureaucratic	Communal	Empowering
	Roles clarified	Roles ambiguous	Roles defined by vision
Social Context	Defined demographically	Defined dialogically	Defined equitably
	Background viewed as excuse for failure	Background adds to school program	Background vital part of ideology
	Orientation: preserving the sta-tus quo	Orientation: accepting of educational change	Orientation: reforming for equity

experts and novices share their prior knowledge and mapping abilities. With guidance from teachers and each other, they learn how to use these cognitive structures to self-regulate and monitor their own thinking. For example, a constructivist learner studying reading and writing would be able to verbalize the purpose of reading and writing and explain several different strategies. Constructivist assessment focuses on evaluation of these cognitive structures and processes instead of attainment of products such as memorized facts.

The critical perspective emphasizes the redistribution of power and instills a sense of social obligation in students. The goal of critical teaching is the development of learners who become empowered themselves or act as advocates for social reforms. Writers on critical teaching (often referred to as critical pedagogy) charge that current teaching transmits a common core of differentially arranged subjects while stressing efficiency and measurement for the primary purpose of maintaining the current social order. Society's goals are maintained primarily through perpetuation of the current curriculum. Several key players in the development of critical pedagogy include John Dewey, Paolo Freire, Peter McLaren, Michael Apple, and Henry Giroux. McLaren (1989) states, "Critical pedagogy is founded on the conviction that schooling for self and social empowerment is ethically prior to mastery of technical skills, which are primarily tied to the logic of the marketplace" (p. 162).

Teaching for Troubled Youth

Often the students who are seen as troubled youth in our schools are also the ones for whom the "one size fits all" model of the functionalist perspective does not work. As Arroyo, Gable, and Selig (this volume) point out, academic failure and student misbehavior often go hand in hand. These authors discuss the academic and behavioral supports that students who cannot fit into the standard curriculum, instructional strategies, and behavior management of the typical classroom seriously need. Theirs is an example of taking a different perspective on teaching.

The educational literature contains numerous case studies, examples, and stories about schools that utilize multiple perspectives. Each school is unique in many ways, but they all share an inclusionary philosophy. The aim of inclusionary schools is to eliminate the labels, categories, and groupings of students that continue to be legal but discriminatory. Examples of such groupings are special education and groupings based on at-risk behaviors. In inclusionary schools, students with troubling behaviors are not removed from classrooms and placed together in special classrooms or in-school suspension rooms. Instruction for all students focuses on individual needs through differentiated instruction. Class and school projects are often designed for social action, such as improvement of a neighborhood playground or publishing a collection of essays and letters on a community concern. The teaching culture in the school is one of critical inquiry in which everyone collaboratively questions the status quo and engages in a quest for alternatives.

There are many ways that current pedagogy can be changed to adapt to the needs of all students. In *Building an Ethical School*, Starratt (1994) suggests that schools should focus teaching about the common good more than they do. He proposes that curricula should address social issues such as the fair distribution of world resources and overcoming disease and unnecessary human suffering. Starratt provides a teaching example using *Goldilocks and the Three Bears* to demonstrate how this goal might be accomplished. The story is traditionally used as a rote language teaching story. However, Starratt suggests that teachers use it to help their students explore perspectives such as that of the bears who have a right to not have their home invaded and that of Goldilocks who saw nothing wrong with her invasion of their home. Consider the possible reactions that these new perspectives on an old story could elicit from various groups of disadvantaged students.

Hurwitz presents another program that is directed at preventing problems encountered by troubled youth. In this volume, Hurwitz outlines a character education model in which school guidance counselors present character lessons through closed circuit television, school events, and extracurricular activities. In this way, guidance counselors become integral to the total school curricular programs and are no longer an isolated part of a separate support system. Also in this volume, Loy and Gregory discuss teaching troubled youth in alternative settings. One can use the multiple perspectives framework to ask questions about alternative settings: What kinds of new and better opportunities do these alternative settings provide for teaching troubled youth? Are alternative settings designed for more constructivist teaching, or are they simply another manifestation of the functionalist perspective to classify and order individuals into the tracks we have decided for them? Are we being critically aware of educating students in a mainstream environment in which they will need to be proficient upon graduation, or are we isolating them for our own convenience which appears easier and more efficient in the short term?

Leadership

The second domain of schools is leadership, and, like teaching, it too can be viewed through a functionalist, constructivist, and critical lens. Functionalist leadership is autocratic. It allocates power to positions within a hierarchical structure for the purpose of maintaining order and the status quo. Therefore, the school principal is placed at the top of the hierarchy and is responsible for all decisions and policies. Individuals are bestowed with power from another who is perceived to be higher in the organizational hierarchy. Decision making is based on policies and procedures, which emphasize equality (equal access) over equity.

In contrast, constructivist leaders redistribute power. Because they see reality as socially created, constructivists view decisionmaking as a collaborative process. Principals work with teachers; they do not mandate to them. The principal is relocated from outside to the center of relationships and functions as a facilitator, change agent, and resource manager. Leadership is distinguished from management and is shared within the school. Collaboration brings new sources of conflict. The constructivist leader recognizes that managed conflict brings diversity of ideas and guides members to understand that, as part of a community, they "agree to disagree" (Lambert, 1995, p. 39). Principals who understand this new source of conflict assist staff by using behaviors that support and stimulate critique, inquiry, innovation, and risk taking in others (Reitzug, 1994b). To facilitate formulation of a shared vision, administrators provide information, establish communication lines and networks, promote teacher development, and obtain and allocate resources according to the boundaries of the vision.

Critical leaders organize their schools around a vision of social reform. Such leadership is "moral" and value driven (Sergiovanni, 1992). It focuses on the examination of power and the elimination of inequities. In critical leadership, power can be exchanged in the form of shared decision making. If shared decision making is authentic, staff members feel ownership and do not see their right to participate as given by a leader who maintains the right to take it back. Many school leaders are now advocating reforms that incorporate shared decision making. However, examination of actual practices often reveals that many of these promises are hollow. Using multiple perspectives as a framework, Reitzug and Capper (1996) analyzed decision making in site-based managed schools. Their findings prompted them to suggest that educators might be "better off under bureaucratic governance than under phony decentralized structures" (p. 66). In other words, leadership that is autocratic and honest about its autocracy is better than a purported democratic process that does not live up to expectations. Others found that educators who work under this inconstancy feel deceived, lose interest in the purported democratic process, and fall back into accepting their powerlessness in a functionalist system (Doyle, 1999; Grant & Sleeter, 1996).

Leadership for Troubled Youth

To meet the needs of troubled youth, schools need to transform. That is, they need to reform not only their structures, but also the thinking behind those structures. Michael Fullan (1993), a nationally known researcher in school reform, argues that for schools to change their practices, leaders cannot mandate but rather must develop the skills, creative thinking, and commitment of others so that they embrace and own the change themselves. The leadership is both from the bottom up and the top down. A contrast of the ethnographical studies of two different schools depicts the kind of transformational leadership that is needed for this change to occur. Both schools were experiments in reform. Both schools held visions of equity for all students. Both schools designed practices and programs to address the needs of troubled students. However, the differences in leadership contributed to the failure of one school and the success of the other.

In the first study, May (1994) tells the story of Richmond Road School where a very charismatic principal and his successor led the school to become internationally known for its successfully reformed program of inclusion. However, May's (1998) follow-up report indicates that this achievement subsequently collapsed because the presiding beliefs of the school belonged to the two dominant administrators rather than to staff members. Teachers and staff members had simply done a good job of implementing the administrators' visions that had been given to them. Although the goals were critically oriented, the leadership remained functionalist in process. The staff's commitment was not to a set of beliefs that they had established but rather to developing the structures for the vision that the administrators had established for them. When these administrators left the school, the visions died.

In contrast, Goodman (1992) told the story of Harmony School where constructivist leaders emphasized incorporating the perspectives of all staff members. The leaders at Harmony School defined organizational functions into "realms of power" and "spheres of influence" so that staff members were authentically engaged in deciding critically oriented goals and strategies that affected their areas of expertise. The staff at Harmony School could not settle into comfortable, unchanging patterns because their leaders stressed the uniqueness of each situation and ongoing dialogue and reevaluation of the ideology. Unlike May's report of the Richmond Road School situation, my personal visit to Harmony School and subsequent references to the school by Goodman (personal communication, 2001) indicated that the leaders and staff at Harmony School continue to collaborate in an ongoing process of clarifying beliefs and fine-tuning structures.

School Organization

The third domain under discussion involves the organization of schools. Of the three types of organizational forms shown in Table 6.1, the functionalist is the one that emphasizes objectivism and determinism. Because functionalists believe that order is maintained through prediction and control, it follows that bureaucracy with its hierarchical structure provides the best organizational form to achieve and maintain this order. Conflicts are resolved through voting in which some participants win, and some lose.

On the other hand, a constructivist view of organizations is more subjective. It recognizes that the individuals involved create social practices. Therefore, a constructivist organization functions collaboratively. Everyone in the organization must have a sense of community and contribute to the ongoing dialogue. Implementation depends on a unified effort. Because, unlike the bureaucracy, roles in this type of organization are not clearly defined, new forms of tension may arise. Stakeholders understand this ambiguity and increase their dialogues in an effort to become a team committed to building a shared vision. Conflicts are resolved through consensus building in which everyone can be satisfied with the outcome.

The third perspective, the critical, adds the belief that "knowledge is power." The purpose of the school organization becomes education for social justice and emancipation of oppressed persons. Although the structures of the critical school may be similar to a constructivist organization, they are driven by a focus on social justice. In an ongoing effort to increase the agency of disempowered groups, members develop strategies to increase awareness of social inequities, and they champion critically oriented issues.

School Organization for Troubled Youth

The story of Harmony School described previously illustrates how a different organizational form can affect how schools deal with troubled youth. For example, Harmony School had guidelines for discipline that focused on its caring community. It did not have inflexible policies that mandated "zero tolerance." Automatized decisions that emerge from narrow functionalist thinking, such as the expulsion of a kindergarten student who brings a squirt gun to school or who raises his or her fingers in the form of a gun, would most likely not occur in Harmony School. Instead, the school as a community would collaboratively design an individualized program to teach the student how the behavior harms the entire community.

Educators, no matter which perspective(s) they use, recognize that there are problems of violence and changing demographics in America's schools. Functionalists clearly recognize the need for schools to be safe places. Their plans to implement safe schools, however, do not include new ideas for transformational change, but rather they consist of layers of the same strategies. The result is increased surveillance of school entrances, overall tightened security, and severe punitive consequences which tend to penalize and further alienate troubled students.

If we continue to view the problem through this narrow lens, we will not achieve safe schools. The problem lies far deeper than the schoolhouse door. Students, the school community, and all educators must change the way we think about schools. These visible bandage approaches may slow the bleeding for only a short time, but the healing must come from within. Clark (this volume) acknowledges the need for heightened security measures but encourages additional perspectives when she guides us to be more alert to the warning signs for violence. She suggests new roles for various staff members who then share in creating atmospheres that prevent violence. Also in this volume are suggestions for how to implement special programs that facilitate development of these preventative atmospheres. The perspectives behind each of these programs go beyond the functionalist view. In this volume, both Forrest and Blagen expand our views by having us develop programs that enter the world of the student to change their lives. Programs such as these "widen our circles" of how we view what the school organization can do to provide unique opportunities of support for troubled youth. They go beyond "more of the same" and transform our thinking not only about what we do, but also why we do it.

Social Context

The fourth and final domain of schools in this framework is social context. Social context refers to the students, families, and other community members who have a direct interest in the role of the school in the development of students and the community. Typically, a school's social context and its impact on schools has been described functionally through demographic facts such as the socioeconomic status of the students' families or the location of the school in an urban, suburban, or rural setting. Although such demographic data provide clear information about schools, they emphasize sameness and include none of the subtleties that make communities unique.

A constructivist perspective recognizes uniqueness and acknowledges that social context adds to the richness of the school program. Constructivist descriptions of the social context go beyond demographic data to illustrate the interaction and dialogical process in which both the school and its social context must participate. Educators have choices in the way that they perceive and interact with their social contexts. Some schools ignore the cultural and social backgrounds of their students, whereas others view them as "cultural capital" (Bourdieu, 1993). Schools operating from a more functionalist perspective might view the backgrounds that poor students bring with them when they enter the school as an excuse for student failure. Schools with a preponderance of constructivist thinking recognize that differences such as race, culture, class, gender, lifestyle, and ability contribute to a desirable pluralistic program. To achieve interaction between the school and the social context, constructivist schools engage in dialogues, which address questions such as, How do we perceive our own needs? What do we perceive are the needs of each other? What do we expect from each other to meet these needs? and How will we work more collaboratively?

The critical perspective adds additional questions to this dialogue. These questions focus on power relationships such as, Who has the power? What will we do about differences in power? What social inequities are present in our school? How will we address these social inequities? and How can our school work toward a vision of social reform, egalitarian values, and the common good?

Social Context for Troubled Youth

The families of many troubled students in our schools are from groups that are disenfranchised from society's educational, economic, political, and social institutions. They are the disempowered without a sense of agency, the "have nots" who are acted upon rather than being initiators because they do not feel empowered to act. They do not challenge their schools or question poor teaching. Schools need to connect with the families of troubled students. Past practices have placed this responsibility on families. However, a multiple perspectives approach recognizes that schools need to take the initiative to make these connections.

In this volume there are several chapters devoted to improving the connections between schools and the social contexts of troubled students. Dorries tells us about the importance of home-school connections to the psychosocial needs of these students. At the same time, however, she warns us that these connections are on the decline. To overcome this discrepancy, Dorries describes methods to encourage home instruction and communication to better link families and schools. Taylor encourages multiple perspectives when he encourages educators to reach out to guardians and parents by "going where they are." From this vantage point, educators see the lives of their students in a new light, one that looks considerably different than the limited view within the schools' walls. And Scaringello brings us full circle by showing us how to use a typically functionalist tool to implement critically oriented goals. Through the computer program called the Cyber-Linkages Model, Scaringello describes how home-school communication linkages can move from telephone calls, newsletters, and PTA meetings to an interactive method in which homes and schools communicate about students' progress, assignments, and other important issues.

CREATING SCHOOLS FOR ALL STUDENTS

Schools for troubled youth need to be "connected" places. Being connected implies that the distinct parts or elements are linked together in a symbiotic relationship and are incapable of being separated. These connections go beyond structures to the perspectives behind them. They go beyond "how we do things" to "why we do them." McAdams and Foster (this volume) call on all educators to consider an "ecological perspective," one that goes beyond the individual and considers multiple environments and factors that affect students. This ecological approach requires a multiplicity of perspectives in how we work with troubled youth.

Making schools equitable for all students will not work until educators recognize, alter, and expand the perspectives behind their actions. Many educators are ready. They are frustrated with current inequitable practices. They see many of the current reform models as isolated add-ons and passing trends that will leave slight imprints on the status quo but will not cause needed systemic change. Many of these educators do not reflect on the perspectives that control their behaviors. Their inability to understand their use of perspectives and to incorporate additional ones locks them into rigid thinking about the teaching, leadership, organization, and social context of their schools.

Reform is facilitated by visionaries, whether they be legislators, administrators, staff members, or parents. What visionaries have in common is the ability to shift perspectives, to question current practice, and to envision alternatives. Reform cannot occur until administrators and educators in the schools have this ability. By wearing multiple lenses, administrators and staff members could view their roles differently and become the visionaries needed by all of the students in their schools.

REFERENCES

Aronowitz, S., & Giroux, H.A. (1991). *Postmodern education: Politics, culture, and social criticism*. Minneapolis: University of Minnesota Press.

Bourdieu, P. (1993). *Sociology in question*. Thousand Oaks, CA: Sage.

Burrell, G., & Morgan, G. (1979). *Sociological paradigms and organizational analysis*. London: Heinemann Press.

Callahan, R.E. (1962). *Education and the cult of efficiency*. Chicago: University of Chicago Press.

Capper, C.A. (1993). Educational administration in a pluralistic society: A multiparadigm approach. In C. A. Capper (Ed.), *Educational administration* (pp. 7–35). Albany: State University of New York (SUNY) Press.

Capper, C.A., Frattura, E., & Keyes, M. (2000). *Meeting the needs of students of ALL abilities: How leaders go beyond inclusion*. Thousand Oaks, CA: Sage.

Denzin, N.K. (1994). The art and politics of interpretation. In N.K. Denzin & Y.S. Lincoln (Eds.), *Handbook of qualitative research* (pp. 500–515). Thousand Oaks, CA: Sage.

Doyle, L. (1999). Leadership and special education reform: Accolades and alarms as accountability constricts intentions. Paper presented at the Annual Meeting of the University Council of Educational Administration, Minneapolis, Minnesota, October 29–31.

Doyle, L.H. (1995). Multiple perspectives: A narrative of special education alternatives. *International Journal of Educational Reform*, 4 (4), 450–459.

Foster, W. (1989). Toward a critical practice of leadership. In W.C. Foster (Ed.), *Critical perspectives on educational leadership* (pp. 39–62). Washington, DC: Falmer Press.

Freire, P. (1970). *Pedagogy of the oppressed*. New York: Continuum.

Fullan, M. (1993). *Change forces*. Philadelphia: Falmer Press.

Goodman, J. (1992). *Elementary schooling for critical democracy*. New York: State University of New York (SUNY) Press.

Grant, C., & Sleeter, C. (1996). *After the school bell rings*. Washington, DC: Falmer Press.

Habermas, J. (1979). *Communication and the evolution of society*. Boston: Beacon Press.

Kegan, R., & Lahey, L. (1984). Adult leadership and adult development: A constructivist view. In B. Kellerman (Ed.), *Leadership: Multidisciplinary perspectives*. Englewood, NJ: Prentice-Hall.

Lambert, L. (1995). Toward a theory of constructivist leadership. In L. Lambert, D. Walker, D.P. Zimmerman, J.E. Cooper, M.D. Lambert, M.E. Gardner, & P.J.F. Slack (Eds.), *The constructivist leader* (p. 199). New York: Teachers College Press.

May, S. (1994). *Making multicultural education work*. Philadelphia: Multilingual Matters Ltd., Ontario Institute for Studies in Education.

May, S. (1998). On what might have been: Some reflections on critical multiculturalism. In G. Shacklock & J. Smyth (Eds.), *Being reflexive in critical educational and social research*. London: Falmer Press.

McAuliffe, G. & Lovell, C. (2000). Encouraging transformation: Guidelines for constructivist and developmental instruction. In G. McAuliffe, K. Eriksen, & Associates (Eds.), *Preparing counselors and therapists: Creating constructivist and developmental programs*. Virginia Beach, VA: Donning Company/Publishers.

McLaren, P. (1989). *Life in schools: An introduction to critical pedagogy in the foundations of education*. New York: Longman.

Reitzug, U.C. (1994a). Diversity, power, and influence: Multiple perspectives on the ethics of school leadership. *Journal of School Leadership, 4* (2), 197–222.

Reitzug, U.C. (1994b). A case study of empowering principal behavior. *American Educational Research Journal, 31* (2), 283–310.

Reitzug, U.C., & Capper, C.A. (1996). Deconstructing site-based management: Possibilities for emancipation and alternative means of control. *International Journal of Educational Reform, 5* (11), 56–69.

Rowan, B. (1995). Learning, teaching, and educational administration: Toward a research agenda. *Educational Administration Quarterly, 31* (3), 344–354.

Sergiovanni, T.J. (1992). *Moral leadership: Getting to the heart of school improvement*. San Francisco: Jossey-Bass.

Sirotnik, K.A., & Oakes, J. (1986). Critical inquiry for school renewal: Liberating theory and practice. In K.A. Sirotnik & J. Oakes (Eds.), *Critical perspectives on the organization and improvement of schooling* (pp. 3–93). Boston: Kluwer-Nijhoff Publishing.

Skrtic, T.M. (1991). *Behind special education: A critical analysis of professional culture and school organization*. Denver, CO: Love Publishing.

Slater, R.O. (1995). The sociology of leadership and educational administration. *Educational Administration Quarterly, 31* (3), 449–472.

Starratt, R.J. (1994). *Building an ethical school: A practical response to the moral crisis in schools*. Washington, DC: Falmer Press.

II

Specific Programs for Work with Troubled Youth in Schools

7

Student Assistance Programs: Accessing Troubled Students' Worlds

Alan Forrest

Today, high school students are bombarded from numerous directions with an almost unmanageable number of demands. They are often overwhelmed with the many choices that they must make on a daily and weekly basis. As counselors, our challenge is to make efforts to connect with these young people. But many do not connect and fall through the cracks. They exist and make it, at least for a period of time, until they attract the attention of a teacher, coach, or principal, and then are referred to the counselor, ostensibly to have the problem "fixed" or "remediated."

And what could the problem(s) be? The primary issues that we see in the schools either directly, or indirectly, revolve around: (1) alcohol and drugs; (2) mental health concerns, such as depression, eating disorders, and anxiety; (3) family (including divorce and discipline); (4) sexual activity and sexually transmitted diseases; and (5) violence (in the school, neighborhood, or community).

There is virtually universal recognition and concern that the earlier an adolescent's troubled world is accessed, the more favorable the outcome. A major goal for educators, therefore, is to address student issues before they become problems and before the student is labeled "at-risk." A Student Assistance Program (SAP) can serve as a mechanism for intervening with students at all of the different stages of the problem continuum.

DESCRIPTION AND RATIONALE FOR SAPs

An SAP is a school-based intervention and prevention program that provides students from kindergarten through college age with information and support for problems associated with alcohol or drug abuse, either their own or that of someone close to them. SAPs are modeled on the highly effective Employee Assistance Programs (EAPs) that have been implemented in the workplace. The mission of an SAP is to work collaboratively with parents and school and community representatives in order to foster resiliency in students and interrupt behaviors that impede students' success. Specific target areas are violence, tobacco, alcohol, other drugs, any difficulties that contribute to truancy, low grades, discipline problems, and the inability to succeed in the educational setting.

Roles

It is important to differentiate between the roles and tasks of school counselors and SAP counselors. Most school personnel, including school counselors, are inundated with a multiplicity of tasks that do not allow for adequate time to dealing with the kinds of complex issues that adolescents present. Addressing such psychosocial difficulties requires a tremendous time commitment if the work is to be done well. Secondary school counselors are traditionally occupied with the following categories of activities: group guidance, career counseling, testing, adjustment concerns, behavioral problems, course scheduling, and other duties as directed by the principal based on the needs of the specific school. School counselors do not have the time to adequately and effectively address students' presenting problems, such as substance abuse and addiction, eating disorders, and family difficulties, in the depth that they require.

An effective SAP will be centered around three specific areas:

1. Prevention, which is the action of deterring children and adolescents who are initially engaging in substance abuse, or engaging in other inappropriate behavior, while they are in school
2. Intervention, which is interceding when alcohol, drugs, or any other behavior is detrimental and may interfere with the lives of the youngsters
3. Follow-up support, which is designed to prevent the relapse, or return, to previously self-destructive behavior (Dean, 1989)

SAPs provide a comprehensive model for the delivery of prevention, intervention, and support services. These services are designed to reduce student risk factors, promote protective elements in students' lives, and increase individual student development.

Components

There are nine SAP components that serve as the minimum requirements deemed necessary to reduce the barriers to learning and assure student success in safe schools and communities. They are school board policy, staff development, program awareness, internal referral process, problem-solving team and case management, student assistance program evaluation, educational student support groups, cooperation and collaboration with community agencies and resources, and integration with other school-based programs. Most, if not all, of these components are illustrated in the vignettes of this chapter and Blagen's description, in the next chapter, of a particular start-up SAP program.

Personnel: The Core Team and the Coordinator

An integral element of any SAP is the effective development and use of a "core team." Core teams are groups of trained teachers and counselors who undertake responsibility for the coordination of services for students. What makes any SAP function is the leadership, which is composed of the core team under the leadership of an SAP coordinator. That individual should possess a background in education or counseling. He or she must assume responsibility for the programming and services to the school. The roles of core teams and SAP coordinators are to disseminate information to students and faculty, identify students who need help, motivate families to look for help, and provide support for students who are trying to make positive changes in their lives.

Although an SAP is an ambitious and comprehensive undertaking, it is possible to "start small." A beginning "core team" needs only two people; the programs that are most effective often start small and grow over time. See Blagen's chapter (this volume) for a description of a start-up small SAP. The core team is a group of school personnel who have been trained to help identify "at-risk" students and to intervene and provide help and support for them. Those at-risk students include, for example, young persons who demonstrate observable behavior that can be attributed to alcohol and drug use, students who may be experiencing poor mental health (depression/anxiety), and students who may have an eating disorder (anorexia/bulimia). Referrals come from teachers, friends, administrators, parents, or anyone who is exposed to the student and notice behaviors that could put the students at-risk.

The Nature of the School-Based SAP

A school-based SAP program, as distinguished from a community agency–based one or a single in-school "alcohol and drug counselor" approach, means that school personnel are trained to provide the direct services to students at the school site. Staff join together to establish a core team at their school, and are responsible for the setting up and running of groups, for disseminating an alcohol and drug abuse curriculum and information on-site, and for making referrals to outside agencies as needed. Most SAP programs do not consider themselves to be treatment programs but rather they see themselves as information and support programs.

Most school staff are already engaged with the behavior and emotional fallout of alcohol and drug abuse in their students, or in their families. An SAP program gives those teachers, counselors, administrators, and clerical staff the tools to be more effective with these individuals. They usually find that once the program is up and running, their time spent doing SAP activities is offset by the time that they no longer have to expend with these students. The advantage of a school-based program is one of ownership and continuity. SAPs are highly utilized by students because they are familiar with the SAP counselors being in the school, and there is no stigma connected to going to see a "substance abuse counselor."

ENTERING TROUBLED STUDENTS' WORLDS WITH AN SAP

Each of the previously identified five "troubled student worlds," that is, those of (1) alcohol and drugs, (2) mental health disorders, (3) family difficulties, (4) sex and sexually transmitted diseases (STDs), and (5) violence will be examined here. I describe actual cases, how they were addressed by an SAP, and how the actions that were taken conceptually conform to the SAP model. In each case, vignette emphasis will be on the identification, intervention, and outcome of the presenting problem.

Alcohol and Drugs

Jimmy was a seventeen-year-old junior who had been drinking and smoking marijuana on a regular basis for the past two years. Recently he had experimented with ecstasy (MDMA) and oxycontin (a widely abused pain-killer). A progression of his chemical use had occurred, and Jimmy had begun to experience negative consequences as a result of his substance abuse. His grades and attendance had fallen significantly, as had his participation in sports. Jimmy displayed an apathetic and disrespectful attitude about almost everything and had socially withdrawn from his good friends of many years. Jimmy was referred to his school's SAP counselor by one of his teachers and the basketball coach after fighting with another student and taking a "swing" at a teacher when he was high. This was his second offense at school as a result of his substance abuse. Instead of the school filing assault charges or school suspension, Jimmy had the choice to meet with an SAP counselor.

Upon referral, Jimmy was resistant and felt that he didn't need to hear what the SAP counselor had to say. The SAP counselor conducted a standard intake interview to obtain information. Jimmy was reluctantly cooperative. He did so only because he knew that if he were not cooperative, he would find himself in juvenile court. Information obtained consisted of substance abuse history, family background, school history, psychosocial assessment, and evaluation of current level of functioning.

The SAP counselor "staffed" Jimmy at a core team meeting later in the week to receive additional information and feedback and to discuss treatment options and recommendations. The general consensus of the core team was that Jimmy was seriously at-risk for continuing to use and abuse, likely to become chemically dependent, and possibly drop out of school. His family history indicated a pattern of substance abuse; with Jimmy's current level of behavior, it was felt that treatment, in the form of counseling, was indicated. Jimmy was to be specifically seen weekly by the SAP counselor for individual counseling and monitoring, but more involvement was felt to be necessary. Once space became available, Jimmy was to participate in an area day treatment program for two weeks. This particular program was coordinated with the school district such that Jimmy could participate and receive academic instruction through some classes and tutoring. His family had been contacted and though somewhat reluctant, did agree for Jimmy to receive help.

Upon completion of the two-week day treatment program, Jimmy was referred to the local mental health center for weekly individual and group counseling. Additionally, he was to attend at least one self-help meeting each week. It was set up with the day treatment program that Jimmy be available for random urine screens. If any returned positive, the SAP counselor and core team would consult, and based on the specifics of the circumstances surrounding Jimmy's return to using, he would immediately be reprimanded to juvenile court with the possibility of being placed in a juvenile detention center.

Mental Health

Mental health concerns of adolescents may take numerous forms, from depression to eating disorders, to anxiety, to low self-esteem, and on and on. The following is a case of individual with an eating disorder. Many adolescent young women are at-risk for eating disorders that are often also associated with low self-esteem. American culture revolves around female thinness and beauty. Simple evidence of this fact is that everyone knows at least one person who is on a diet. In a recent poll by *People* magazine, 80% of women reported that the images of women on TV, movies, fashion magazines, and advertising make them feel insecure about their looks. Data reported by the American Psychiatric Association suggest that, of all psychiatric disorders, the greatest degree of patient mortality due to natural and unnatural causes is associated with eating disorders and substance abuse.

Mary was an eighteen-year-old high school senior. She regularly ate huge amounts of food, and purged several times a day. Each day she would resolve not to continue in her binge/purging behavior, yet every day she would find herself purchasing large amounts of junk food and eventually searching for a restroom. She'd cry and beg herself to stop. Mary did not feel good about herself as a daughter, student, friend, or person in general, and her family was both appalled by and concerned about her behavior. She kept asking herself, "Why do I do this crazy behavior over and over again?" There are many theories and attempts to explain this behavior, such as fear of becoming a woman, control issues, societal pressures to be thin, anger, resentment, and unresolved grief over the loss of a loved one.

Had it not been for several of Mary's friends who were concerned over her deteriorating physical appearance, Mary might have become just another statistic, someone else who died from this debilitating disorder. But her friends contacted the school counselor, who in turn made a referral to the SAP counselor. With a reluctant commitment, Mary agreed to see the SAP counselor. Upon initial intake, it was rapidly determined that Mary was bulimic and at risk for serious health problems. Mary's parents were contacted and brought into the SAP counselor's office for a subsequent family counseling session. The core team assessed the case and made the recommendation for Mary to not be permitted to return to school until she received a thorough medical evaluation from her family physician. This assessment was performed, and her doctor decided to immediately hospitalize Mary because of her significant weight loss.

Upon Mary's return to school, she was placed in a weekly young women's self-esteem group that was led by the SAP counselor. The range of topics discussed in this group included self-esteem issues, depression, developmental concerns, dating, family issues, and eating disorders. Mary received the support from the group, scheduled individual meetings with the SAP counselor when warranted, and was monitored by her family doctor. What made the case of Mary successful was that the SAP counselor both had the time and was knowledgeable in effectively facilitating a successful intervention.

Family Dysfunction

The causes for adolescents' acting out behavior (which can range from mild to moderate to severe) are frequently, if not always, related to dysfunctional family dynamics and patterns of interaction. Such dynamics, combined with numerous other social variables (peer influences and the media), can result in many forms of inappropriate or maladaptive behavior. It is not unusual to discover multiple problems existing within families. Often we find that, right below the surface, hidden from friends, teachers, coaches, clergy, and other significant persons, there are family difficulties that are not easily discernable. The adolescent then becomes the "scapegoat," that is, the member of the family who attracts attention to the fact that something is wrong. Many helping professionals who may not have adequate training in working with adolescents and families experience difficulty in helping in this area.

Jordan was a six-foot, six-inch sixteen-year-old high school junior who was failing several subjects, which jeopardized his sports eligibility. He was a star player on the basketball team; there he received much attention and validation as a person. As a result of his poor grades, and the possibility of becoming ineligible to play basketball, Jordan presented at times as being quite depressed. A teacher who had taken an interest in Jordan referred him to the SAP counselor knowing that "something wasn't right," but was unsure of what to do about it.

During the initial SAP interview, Jordan, though originally reluctant to talk about what was going on, eventually disclosed that he was extremely fearful that his parents were going to get divorced. He was also apprehensive about sharing this concern with the counselor because of being perceived as not being loyal to the family by breaking the family code of silence. Jordan reported that there was a tremendous amount of conflict between his parents and that there were occasional times when his father struck his mother.

Jordan's parents were both laborers who worked hard to make ends meet for Jordan and his two younger siblings. Jordan's father had a bad temper and frequently argued with him, telling him that the only way he could succeed was to receive a basketball scholarship and make a better life for himself and for the entire family. His mother was the peacemaker in the family and usually sided with Jordan against his father, which exacerbated the problems between his parents.

The SAP counselor felt that there were significant family systems issues occurring. He requested that Jordan ask his parents if they would be willing to come to school for a family counseling session. The family was initially opposed to meeting with the counselor. It wasn't until the mother threatened to leave the relationship that father reluctantly agreed to the family meeting.

Throughout the session Jordan's parents wanted to keep the focus on him and his problems. It became apparent to the SAP counselor that there was a significant power struggle occurring between the parents themselves. They would frequently engage Jordan in a triangulated position. There were poor patterns of communication, parenting and discipline differences, and spousal disagreement over which course of action to take with the children. And, of course, there was the issue of the father's temper, the physical abuse directed toward the mother, and the emotional abuse directed toward the children. Such a labyrinth required intensive intervention.

Over the period of about one month and three family counseling sessions with the SAP counselor, Jordan's parents became aware of the relationship between the behavior at home and Jordan's problems at school. However, further family work was not possible, for, even though SAP counselors typically do have a working knowledge of family systems and dynamics, they simply do not have the time to engage in ongoing family counseling sessions. Because of the physical and emotional abuse, the core team discussed the necessity of contacting Social Services to investigate. It was decided that Social Services be contacted (which would put pressure on the family to follow through on all treatment recommendations). Additionally, a referral was made to an area family therapist for ongoing family work. Jordan was also to meet with the SAP counselor on a weekly basis for individual counseling. The SAP counselor and family therapist were to talk monthly to consult on the progress of the family and of Jordan.

Sexual Behavior

Many American young people begin having sexual intercourse during adolescence. In recent years there has been a substantial increase in the proportion of adolescents who report sexual activity at each year of age during adolescence. Initial sexual intercourse experiences are usually important (and sometimes defining) events in the lives of young people. The beginning of sexual activity is meaningful for several reasons. First, the younger the age of first sexual intercourse, the more likely that the experience will have been coercive. Such forced sexual intercourse is related to long-lasting negative effects on relationships and intimacy in adulthood. Second, the younger the age of first sexual intercourse, the greater the risk of unwanted pregnancy and STDs. This consequence occurs because those who begin having sex at young ages are less likely to use contraception, they generally have more sexual partners, and they tend to engage in higher risk sexual behaviors such as alcohol or drug use prior to sexual intercourse and having multiple concurrent sexual partners.

Michelle was an attractive seventeen-year-old high school junior who lived with her mother and nineteen-year-old sister. Her father had left the family when Michelle was seven and had had little contact with them since. Michelle's sister introduced her to marijuana when she was fourteen, and Michelle could be described as a casual marijuana user who also drank at parties on weekends. Michelle tended to "hang out" with her sister's friends, who were generally two to five years older.

Michelle's initial sexual experience had occurred when she was fifteen. She was at a party where she had been smoking marijuana and drinking. She ended up having sex with an eighteen-year-old friend of her sister. The entire experience was unpleasant and left Michelle feeling empty and used. However, she was one of the first in her peer group to lose her virginity and was rewarded with lots of attention at school.

Over the following two years, Michelle had had four different sexual partners, but would not have described herself as promiscuous. Sex became just another part of the dating process, something to do on a Saturday night. It was relatively uneventful. However, one weekend she met a twenty-one-year-old friend of her sister at a party. They engaged in sexual intercourse, but this time it became dangerous for Michelle because the man she was with became abusive and violent.

Over the weekend she told her mother she was sick and stayed in her room. Michelle did not return to school until Tuesday, hoping her bruises would have partially healed. Her physical education teacher saw her in second period, talked with her, and referred her to the SAP counselor at the school. Because Michelle was a quiet, well-behaved student who received Bs and Cs, she was the type of person who did not receive the attention of teachers. Upon entering the office of the SAP counselor, Michelle presented as being very quiet and withdrawn. The makeup she tried to use to cover her bruises was not working.

Although reticent and reluctant to report what had happened, eventually Michelle began weeping and told the SAP counselor the entire story. In her own mind, Michelle did not see how she had been sexually assaulted. After much talk, Michelle agreed to see a doctor at the local Women's Resource Center, but only if her mother would not be informed about what had happened. The SAP counselor facilitated the appointment and went with her to the center the following day.

The physical examination revealed that Michelle had herpes and had probably had it for the past six to twelve months. She needed treatment and would need to talk with her mother, but was extremely frightened to do so. The SAP counselor contacted her mother and scheduled a family session. At that meeting Michelle informed her mother about what had happened. Both Michelle, her sister, and her mother were then referred to a family counselor in the community. In addition, Michelle began a weekly group counseling session at the school facilitated by the SAP counselor. The group consisted of juniors and seniors who were coping with self-esteem, substance abuse, and relationship issues.

Michelle also received treatment for her herpes, attended weekly group counseling sessions, and went to family therapy once every two weeks with her mother. She attended a two-day substance abuse program in the school upon the recommendation of the core team. Her mother now tried to monitor her more carefully. Michelle met with the SAP counselor for individual "check-in" meetings once a week for about fifteen to thirty minutes. Using the ecological model (McAdams & Foster, this volume), teachers sent weekly assignment and grade reports to the counselor. A comprehensive treatment plan was developed in collaboration with Michelle. Within three months, she began to feel better about herself and had become a solid B student in school.

Violent Behavior

There is extensive concern about the apparent increased incidence of violent behavior among adolescents as evidenced by the recent plague of school shootings over the past five years. This complex and troubling issue needs to be carefully understood by all involved: parents, teachers, counselors, other adults, and students themselves. Violent behavior in adolescents can include a wide range of expressions: explosive temper tantrums, physical aggression, fighting, threats or attempts to hurt others (including homicidal thoughts), use of weapons, cruelty toward animals, fire setting, intentional destruction of property, and vandalism.

Tucker was a seventeen-year-old white male high school student who experienced a tremendous amount of isolation and rejection from his peer group. He grew up in an abusive home environment; his father was a retired Marine sargeant and veteran of the Gulf War, and his mother was a passive, closet alcoholic. His father often watched violent and pornographic videos at home. He had a violent temper, a military gun collection, and was physically abuse to Tucker, his younger brother, and his mother. His father's motto was "spare the rod and spoil the child." As a result Tucker was the recipient of frequent physical abuse by his father and neglect from his mother

Tucker would retreat to his bedroom and draw and spend a lot of time on the Internet; his favorite Web sites were survivalist sites that explained how he could "make it on his own." They advised about how corrupt the government had become and how it "used" citizens for its own purposes. Tucker had recently begun drinking with his only two friends, who shared similar sentiments about the government and about how crazy the world was becoming. Alcohol was the only substance that Tucker used, not wanting to become involved with the type of people who bought and used drugs, believing that they were part of the problem of what was wrong with this country.

In school, Tucker presented as quiet and withdrawn. He was a C and D student. What brought Tucker to the attention of school personnel was an incident in which some of his graphically violent drawings fell out of his book bag in class. A few of the girls in the class saw them and reported him to the teacher, who in turn sent him to the principal's office. Once there, Tucker barely said a word. When questioned about his drawings, which depicted a young man shooting teachers at the school, Tucker did not respond at all to the principal. The principal, very concerned over what he saw, called the SAP counselor to his office, explained the situation, and left them alone to talk.

The counselor conducted a thorough intake interview and learned about Tucker's family. She presented the case of Tucker at the next core team meeting. It was recommended that he receive a thorough psychiatric evaluation. This was done only after his mother secretly signed the consent form providing permission for the evaluation (his father would not sign the form nor agree to the evaluation). The evaluation revealed a very depressed young man with a tremendous amount of unexpressed anger directed toward his parents and other authority figures. It was suggested that Tucker receive individual and family counseling. The family counseling never occurred, but over time Tucker did respond to the individual counseling with the SAP counselor whom he trusted.

The counseling sessions addressed Tucker's depression and family issues. This work averted what could have been another tragic school shooting or adolescent suicide. The SAP counselor responded to the issues posed by Tucker by addressing family dynamics, stressors, dysfunctional attitudes, and inappropriate discipline. Failure to adequately address all of Tucker's issues could have put himself, the school, and others at serious risk.

POLICIES THAT ENSURE THE SUCCESS OF AN SAP

Each of the vignettes describes methods that SAP counselors can use to intervene and effectively address issues for adolescents who are at-risk. To some degree all adolescents are at-risk, and there needs to be a mechanism to address the many issues that adolescents are confronted with in the schools of the twenty-first century.

In order for SAPs to be effective, there must be support from school board members and through written policy. Such a policy is designed to validate the creation of SAPs and notify the community that improper behavior by students will be addressed. The policy should also express that:

1. The school is committed to students achieving their full potential.
2. Inappropriate student behavior deters adolescents from attaining their full potential.
3. SAPs that focus on prevention and intervention activities are necessary to help students develop their full potential. (Dean, 1989)

SUMMARY AND FUTURE DIRECTIONS

Most schools are overburdened with maladaptive behavior and emotional fallout from countless sources, including dysfunctional families or families who are just trying to "make it" in a society that places ever-changing demands on students, teachers, school counselors, parents, school administrators, treatment personnel, and community resources. An SAP provides all who are concerned with students the tools to be more effective with them. Once an SAP has been established, the time spent engaged in SAP activities is easily justified by contrast to the previously ineffective time spent in futile attempts at remediation, punishment, and damage control.

As illustrated in the vignettes, a school-based SAP consists of trained school personnel who provide direct services to students at the school setting. Teachers, counselors, staff, administrators, and community resources come together to establish a core team at their school. This group of concerned individuals is responsible for the organizing and facilitation of counseling groups, for disseminating an alcohol and drug abuse curriculum and information on-site, and for making referrals to outside agencies as needed. Most SAP programs do not provide long-term treatment but rather emphasize information giving, problem identification, referral, and support.

A major advantage of a well-functioning SAP includes its being highly utilized by students because the SAP counselors are known to them as affiliated with their school. Teachers and other school personnel are more likely to make referrals to SAP counselors because they are known and relationships have been developed. The information and groups provided by the SAP are available to all students. Additionally, there may be less of a stigma in seeing an SAP counselor, as opposed to a mental health clinician who periodically comes to the school and is available for students. A final advantage lies in the sense of continuity and decreased likelihood of the program dissolving when one person leaves, due to staff being trained in an ongoing way.

Any approach examining the issues of students who are at-risk must be practical and effective. Although SAPs are not the sole remedy for all that ails schools, they can serve as a central and fundamental intervention, one that appears to be more effective than other school-based intervention programs for at-risk adolescents. By empowering schools to build on the resources that already exist—students, parents, teachers, guidance counselors, and school administrators—SAPs can provide leadership for identifying, intervening, treating, and supporting all students in schools.

It is worth stating that "no single strategy has demonstrated long-term impact" (Wallack & Corbett, 1990, p. 15) on at-risk adolescents, whether the issue is substance abuse, sexual behavior, or identification of potentially violent individuals. Identifying, intervening, treating, and supporting students, regardless of their individual issue, is a shared responsibility among all who interact with the specific student. Although we will likely never fully prevent or end troubled student worlds (those of alcohol and drugs, mental health disorders, family difficulties, sex and STDs, and violence), it is necessary for schools not to "bury their heads in the sand." A preferred path to follow is development of an SAP that effectively generates plans and preparations for the psychosocial disruptions of what really exists.

REFERENCES

Dean, O.A. (1989). *Facing chemical dependency in the classroom with student assistance programs*. Deerfield Beach, FL: Health Communications, Inc.

Wallack, L., & Corbett, K. (1990). *Illicit drug, tobacco and alcohol use among
       youth: Trends and promising approaches in prevention.* (Office for Sub-
       stance Abuse Prevention Monograph 6). Washington, DC: U.S. De-
       partment of Health and Human Services, Public Health Service.

8

The Birth and Growth of a Student Assistance Program: A Case Study

Mark Blagen

The problem is obvious: too many students bring personal problems to school, ones that often (but not always) manifest themselves in poor academic progress, a lethargic attitude, inconsistent attendance, disruptive behavior, and self-destructive tendencies. In most schools the percentage of students who have these problems could easily approach 25% (Anderson, 1988).

What is a school to do? The answer most likely will not be found by turning to the guidance department. Most states mandate that a secondary school counselor's case load be 250–400 students. Although school counselors are the ones who are ostensibly trained to work with the myriad of problems facing adolescents, they usually are barely able to provide the needed developmental services to this caseload and to react to crisis situations. Their ability to attend to problems in their more manageable infancy and to work with a student on a continuing basis is severely limited.

In this chapter I echo the call initiated by Alan Forrest in this volume for establishing Student Assistance Programs (SAPs) in order to respond to the needs of all public school students. Described here is my and my colleagues' recent experience in initiating an SAP model.

The power of an SAP lies in its inclusion of all stakeholders: parents, students, administrators, guidance counselors, and teachers. I share my own experience as a professional who participated in creating an SAP. I then present five specific examples of how an SAP can make a difference in the lives of individual students. I conclude by addressing more broadly based, systemic issues. I hope that these descriptions might serve as an inspiration and possible model for implementing such a program.

PREPARATION FOR THE PROGRAM

When I and another experienced counselor were originally contracted to establish an SAP model for a school system, we quickly learned that, in practice, a standardized SAP model does not exist. By studying numerous school systems, we discovered that this tends to be a catch-all concept. For example, many programs were "partial," in that they focused on only some of the needs of some of the students mentioned earlier. For example, one program that was often referred to as a "model" program was severely underfunded: It was a single SAP that attempted to respond to the needs of two large high schools (a total of over 4,000 students). Although this program was an exemplar in how it was run, its effectiveness was severely limited by its inability to respond to many students in need.

We also found, in our research, that sometimes these programs were reactive—only responding to acute circumstances such as an increase of suicide attempts in a particular district or at a particular school. Thus, there were almost always specific problems that a particular SAP responded well to, such as smoking cessation or conducting a group to assist student-mothers finish high school. Typically, however, there were other problems or programs that the SAP did not respond well to, such as working with students who had returned to school after being treated for a substance abuse problem.

Early on, we were informed that school administrators were concerned about community acceptance of SAPs. They were wary of the anti-school counseling element in the local community. That group had in the recent past been very active. Would they vocalize their opposition to any new program that increased the school role in students' psychosocial adjustment? For this reason, and to more closely align this program with other alternative education initiatives in our district, we renamed our program the "Student Support Program." The following is a brief description of this program. It has parallels to the SAP that was described and defined in Forrest's chapter in this volume. This description, however, emphasizes the start-up dimensions of an SAP.

DESCRIPTION OF THE STUDENT SUPPORT PROGRAM

The Context: Alternative Education Programs

The Student Support Program that is described here was designed to be a component of a broader Alternative Education Program plan, as these programs often are. The Alternative Education Program plan in this district was a school board–approved, five-year master plan aimed at developing effective alternatives for school youth. As with the Student Support Program, the Alternative Education Program has elements that are both proactive and reactive. Both the Alternative Education Program and the Student Support Programs are designed to be incrementally implemented, with the goal of providing comprehensive services over time.

The Student Support Program was an integral part of this school's guidance department and worked closely with the school administration, faculty, and parents in identifying and removing barriers that impede student success. Again, as iterated by McAdams and Foster, and also by Clark in this volume, the ecological/collaborative approach to student development guided us. The success of a program such as this rests in its ability to be both a "stand-alone" effort and an integrated part of both the guidance and administrative structure of a school.

Target Populations

The Student Support Program was designed to respond systematically to high-risk students. For the purpose of this program, "high-risk student" was defined as any student who was at risk of dropping out of school, becoming involved in the problematic use of alcohol or other drugs, or becoming involved in any violent, risky, or self-destructive behavior. The broad nature of this definition allowed the program to potentially include all students.

Functions of the Student Support Program

The two basic functions of this Student Support Program, and most such programs, were to provide both prevention *and* early intervention services to students who were having academic or behavioral difficulties. Referral for these services was made by faculty, administrators, guidance counselors, and parents and by the students themselves. Referrals were handled sensitively and confidentially.

Program services included the presentation of drug education, teaching coping and problem-solving skills, conducting anger management groups, facilitation of conflict resolution, doing crisis intervention, and teaching stress management strategies. These topics were presented in individual and small-group focus sessions, as well as through classroom presentations.

The Program's Evolution

Funding

Initially, federal "Safe and Drug-Free Schools and Communities" grant funding was used to seed this program. Money from this grant was allocated for two twenty-hour positions. One position was located at a feeder middle school, and one position was located at the selected high school.

First Year

Due to the incremental nature of implementation, the first year was primarily one for program development. The initial program development efforts included informing the teachers, administrators, and students of the potential of the program, as well as its components and intents. My being in the hallways, interacting with the students and teachers, and being an integral part of the environment laid the foundation for the students and teachers to accept this program. Because of my presence and my extensive visits to classrooms, students generally saw being referred to me as an opportunity to be helped and not as a punishment.

Implementation Plan

Most of the participants were part of the "vast middle," that is, these students' needs would not be attended to until a crisis occurred. This population is in essence "hidden." This is so not because teachers or others did not recognize these students as experiencing problems, but because there were not resources to assist these students. As mentioned earlier, the Student Support Program was originally designed to be in one high school (grades 9–12 with 2,300 students) on a part-time basis (only twenty hours a week) and one feeder middle school. The low referral numbers of the inception year was due to the program not commencing until the fourth week of school, and was reflective of the newness of the program and its part-time availability. During the second year, due to the obvious need, the program was expanded to a full-time basis.

Table 8.1 shows that, as the program was implemented, referrals from counselors, teachers, and administrators increased dramatically.

This increase was primarily due to a shift from a part- to a full-time program and the success of program development. As the program became

Table 8.1
Referral by Nine-Week Period for the First and Second Year

First Year	1st Nine Weeks	2nd Nine Weeks	3rd Nine Weeks	4th Nine Weeks
# of referrals	7	9	16	10
Second Year	1st Nine Weeks	2nd Nine Weeks	3rd Nine Weeks	4th Nine Weeks
# of referrals	26	26	31	22

more developed, referrals from teachers increased as they were sensitized to students who are experiencing a problem. The referrals that came from teachers tended to often be vague and complex. Several of these referrals communicated the teacher's "feelings" that a student was experiencing some sort of difficulty. What the teachers usually observed was related to a significant change in affect or academic performance. As shown below, most referrals came from the guidance counselors.

The primary type of problems that students experienced is indicated in Table 8.2. It can be seen that the school counselor is a central figure in referring troubled students.

Most students referred were experiencing more than one problem, but what is listed in Table 8.3 indicates the primary reason for referral. Many of these students were initially not able to verbalize what was causing the change, but as they felt more comfortable with me, they slowly began to share what they were experiencing.

After two years, we asked, "How effective was this program?" The following section looks at this question. In addition, five case examples that demonstrate its impact are presented.

PROGRAM IMPACT

The Difficulty of Measuring Large-Scale Impact

Although this program had been in effect for only two years, it was clear that it had had a positive impact on individual students. But what about its larger impact on the school? Attempting to measure this impact is much more difficult to determine. Over time we had hoped that we would see that overall attendance rates had improved, or that suspensions had

Table 8.2
Referral by Source, First and Second Year

	First Year	Second Year
Counselor	19	47
Teacher	8	20
Parent	7	10
Self	5	6
Administrator	1	15
Substance abuse program staff	2	5
Resource officer	1	1
Peer	0	1

Table 8.3
Referral by Type of Problem, First and Second Year

	First Year	Second Year
Alcohol or other drug	14	38
Anger control	12	26
Academic motivation	8	20
Family of origin issues	4	7
Suicide ideation/depression	4	11
Grief	1	1
Stress	0	2

dropped, or the drop-out rate had decreased. We were concerned that, if the attendance rates did not show improvement and the drop-out rate remained unchanged, support for the program would diminish. Would that mean that the program had not helped or was worth the expenditure?

We could not show that large-scale impact. Anecdotal data had to suffice. For example, I am quite certain that, in the first year of the program, two seniors graduated who would not have, had they not been referred to this program. I am also certain that several others did not graduate because they were not referred. Thus, even though this program likely made a difference in those two individuals who did graduate, that difference could not translate into larger, measurable systemic impact.

A second difficulty in demonstrating impact is the fact that individual change may take place some time after the intervention. For example, a referred student may still make the decision to drop out, but as a direct result of the intervention, soon decide to obtain a high school equivalency degree and attend a community college and eventually a university. Another example of the difficulty in determining systemic impact is that Student Support Program staff may make many referrals to other alternative education programs such as the Substance Abuse Intervention Program (SAIP) or Suspension Intervention Program (SIP). These referrals may be construed by district or school administrators as the Student Support Program's not being effective, when in fact the opposite may be true. By making referrals to the SIP and SAIP, the Student Support Program assisted these students to receive needed services. What actually happened in the first two years of the Student Support Program was that referrals to the SIP and SAIP did increase. There were two factors responsible for this. The first was that as a direct result of the Student Support Program, more students in need of these programs were identified and referred. Second, there was less of a tendency to ignore or cover up problems because now these students could be referred to the Student Support Program.

The systemic impact of this program may never be demonstrated due to the above and other factors. However, we could evaluate whether we impacted the target group, that is, those students who were at risk of dropping out or who were involved in self-destructive behavior. We can evaluate whether we made a difference in the lives of the individuals in that group.

Toward that end, detailed below are the cases of five students who benefited from this program. Names and identifying information have been changed. These five cases are typical ones. Each illustrates some of the different kinds of problems that students brought to the Student Support Program.

Mandy—From a Difficult Beginning to a Promising Future

This case illustrates the significant difference that early intervention can make. Mandy was a very bright, hardworking ninth-grade student who began experiencing significant behavioral problems during her last year in middle school. During that year, she had had thirteen behavioral referrals. Her normal B average had also slid to a low C. From all indications, Mandy was headed for a difficult ninth grade year. During the first week of high school, Mandy was referred by her first period teacher to the Student Support Program specialist for threatening to "take a classmate's head off" and making derogatory remarks toward another student. Mandy was challenged by me to look at her behavior and decide if this was the way to get her needs met. Mandy quickly decided that it was not really how she wanted to begin her high school years. She had learned in her family that the best way to get her needs met was through intimidation and anger. Mandy had two older siblings that had been very involved in the criminal justice system and she felt that she was destined to follow their lead.

We discussed discovering more appropriate ways to get her needs met, and Mandy stated that she felt these alternate ways would benefit her. By the end of her third session, Mandy and I both felt that she was competent in identifying her own negative acting-out behaviors and using the alternate behaviors that she had identified. I kept in close contact with her referring teacher, and all indications were that she had made a complete turnaround.

By the end of the first nine-week term, she had been recommended to be moved into Honors English. Mandy received one of two As that her teacher gave to his Honors English class for the semester. At the end of the first semester, Mandy was on the honor roll. However, her behavior did regress somewhat during the second semester, due to substantial stressors at home. It was not unusual for Mandy to discuss extended family members who had been put in jail or, in one case, murdered. Mandy had a tendency to *react* to the slightest provocation instead of "acting." She quickly grasped the distinction and would often share examples of how she acted instead of reacted. We also began to discuss and consider what factors in her home environment she could control, and what factors she could not.

Mandy demonstrated significant academic and behavioral improvement during this important ninth-grade transition year. This behavioral change set the tone for the possibility of substantial success in high school. Mandy is one of those students "in the middle" who would have previously been ignored and tolerated until her behavior became a discipline issue. Her grades would have most likely continued to remain far below her potential. She probably would have dropped out within a couple of years due to her home environment, which was one that did not encourage her academically. Her academic success and the encouragement she received from teachers, administrators, and counselors gave her a new perspective, one in which she could see that she was an academically capable student and that attending a university had relevance to her.

Charlene—Wounded by Her Alcoholic Mother

Many students experience school as a refuge from the chaos they experience at home. Some students respond to their home dysfunction by overachievement in school or school-related activities. For others this dysfunction and chaos manifests in depression, anxiety, anger, the self-destructive use of psychoactive substances or sex, and other acting-out behaviors. Charlene was a withdrawn student and her "problems" were not easily detected by her teachers. If they were asked, her teachers would have described Charlene as a quiet underachiever. Luckily, there was an adult in Charlene's life, namely, the school "resource officer," who did notice a dramatic change in her affect and who did something about it.

Referrals can come from virtually anyone. I had approached our resource officer early in the first year, knowing that he could be a valuable source for referrals. A resource officer is a uniformed police officer assigned to the school on a full-time basis to provide community policing services. Charlene was referred to me within days of my introduction to him. She was exhibiting what appeared to the resource officer as being a severe, negative mood swing. This student had built rapport with the resource officer, and the sudden mood swing concerned him. In the first session that I saw her, it was clear that the student's mother was an alcoholic and, even though the student lived with her father, the mother's behavior continued to have an enormous impact on her. Charlene was already in private counseling for a previous depressive episode.

Charlene responded very well in weekly problem-solving sessions with the student support specialist. In the beginning, she had difficulty understanding that she had any power in her relationship with her mother. Understanding the power that she had became much easier as she began to understand more about her mother's alcoholism. She recognized that her mother's behavior had very little to do with her. Charlene's grades dramatically increased from a D average in the second nine-week period, to a C average in the third nine weeks, to a solid B average and the honor roll for the fourth nine weeks.

Through our sessions, Charlene learned that it was her responsibility to define her boundaries in her relationship with her mother and to be assertive in her behavior toward her. During the last few minutes of each session, we would discuss her academic progress. This was something the meant a great deal to her, and she was very proud of her recent progress.

During the following school year, Charlene continued to see the student support specialist approximately once every two weeks for various problems related to the negative impact her noncustodial mother continued to have. But most often, I just listened and would simply ask her questions like, What does all this mean to you? or How could you have handled that situation differently? Asking these questions had a positive impact on her. She used the sessions to verbalize her concerns and was challenged to continue to take full responsibility for what she could control—her thoughts, feelings, and behavior. She continues to be academically successful by remaining on the honor roll for both the first and second semesters. Charlene would most likely continue to be supported on a less frequent basis in her final years of high school due to her continual maturation and ability to handle this stressful and painful situation with her new insight and understanding.

Paul—From Addiction to Recovery

Often, students involve themselves with psychoactive drugs in a way that is not just a phase or experimentation, but that is much more problematic. These students will disguise their use by maintaining the façade of normal activity and behavior. Inevitably, the student will find this façade more and more difficult to maintain. The response to these students by teachers, administrators, and parents is generally punitive in nature. Punitive sanctions will usually create some motivation (challenge) for change, but without treatment (support) of some kind, there will be little chance of any real change of behavior. Paul is a rather typical example of a student experiencing problematic use of marijuana.

Paul was a junior who was referred to the student support specialist by a teacher, due to a dramatic decline in his academic motivation and performance. Paul was relatively honest about his involvement with marijuana and admitted that it was causing some problems. However, he was not motivated to do anything about his problem. His parents were informed and given several helping resources. They declined to take any action. Paul's behavior continued to decline to the point at which he was being considered, because of truancy and disrespectful behavior, for an alternative school placement. Because Paul was taking four advanced placement courses, his guidance counselor argued that Paul would not be able to establish enough credit to graduate with his class; these courses were not offered at the alternative school.

Upon our urging, Paul's parents had him admitted to an intensive outpatient adolescent treatment program. Paul initially did well in staying away from drug-using friends, but this lasted for only a few weeks. Once again he began skipping classes and associating with his previous friends. Based on the recommendation of the principal, one last intervention was attempted.

This time Paul became motivated to change. Initially, he would visit my office on a nearly daily basis. He described how difficult it was to stay away from marijuana and how he would crave using it. I listened and assisted him in developing strategies. I suggested that he "think his craving through." I asked if he were to act on craving, What would it mean? He found this suggestion to be very helpful. He also began to identify his support systems and became willing to use these when he was bored, feeling down, or wanted to use. He listened to my suggestions and each day would report to me what seemed to help. Within a month, his daily visits began to have a different tone. His affect was upbeat, and he would share with me poetry or lyrics that he had written. He also met his first nondrug-using girlfriend during this time. Paul finished out the year on the honor roll, reached the top 10% on his college aptitude tests, and was looking forward to his senior year. He was now clearly a competitive candidate at a selective university. Paul would not have done well without the support that he got from the formal structure of the Student Support Program.

John—Being Cared for Makes a Difference

As with adults, many students who are involved in problematic use of psychoactive substances have very little hope in their life. Assisting these students to recover that hope was always one of my goals. Sometimes recovering hope was very difficult and in all cases challenging. In John's case I had some excellent assistance, and we were successful.

In November of the first year of the Student Support Program, this author gave a prevention-oriented presentation to all of the ninth-grade health classes. This presentation consisted of fifty minutes of interaction with the students. There were three purposes to this discussion. The first was to allow the students to understand their responsibility in making decisions about their use of psychoactive substances. This was done by discussing what psychoactive substances do to the central nervous system; the addictive nature of psychoactive substances, including marijuana; and how the use of psychoactive substances interferes with normal adolescent processes such as the development of achievement motivation. The second purpose was to explore the various reasons that some students might not graduate from high school, what they could do to prevent this from occurring, and how not graduating was related to the decisions that they were currently making. The third purpose was to introduce myself and the services of the Student Support Program so that students were aware of its services. I always finished my presentation by inviting them to see me if their report card did not reflect the grades that they wanted to get. It was a safe reason for approaching me.

Within a week after this presentation, John referred himself for what he described as his "overinvolvement with marijuana." I saw John for about six sessions during that school year. During these sessions we would discuss his progress toward not using marijuana and other decisions he was making. Much progress was made initially. In accordance with school board policy, I could only see a student three times before parental permission had to be obtained. I informed John in our first session that I would need to speak with his foster mother after our third session. John was present when I called her and explained why I was working with John. She was relieved and seemed very motivated to do anything that she could. I recommended that she take John to a counselor for a substance abuse assessment. I gave her a list of counselors who were experienced in providing this service. She soon followed up on this recommendation, and John began attending a weekly substance abuse group under the supervision of a private, certified substance abuse counselor.

Close to the end of that school year, it was obvious that John was losing his motivation to stay away from marijuana and alcohol. This concern was shared with his foster mother, who concurred that John was regressing. At the beginning of the next school year, I attempted to locate John during his "resource period." John was receiving special education services for a learning disability. His resource period was part of his special education individualized education plan. However, he was not with his resource teacher whenever I attempted to locate him. He was skipping class. I briefly explained who I was to his resource teacher. I caught up with him during a class that he was regularly attending.

Our first encounter that year was not pleasant. He was aloof and defensive. These were traits that I had not observed in him previously. He had been in trouble in the summer and had been arrested on possession of alcohol and had left home for a period of time. He was not doing well at this time.

John began to see that his resource teacher, myself, and his foster mother were not going to give up on him. When John realized this, he began to regain hope and began to make excellent progress.

It was also during this time frame that John asked about the Commonwealth Challenge Program. This was a volunteer "boot-camp" type of alternative education program operated by the state. It was designed for students who had dropped out of high school. After viewing a videotape and attending an informational session concerning the Commonwealth Challenge Program, he became motivated to be accepted into that program. John was able to meet the requirements of the program, ones that included being drug free and having the possession charge dropped. He responded exceedingly well to the rigors of the Commonwealth Challenge Program and was at the top of his class in several categories and near the top in most other categories. He has since received his GED. Due to his learning disability, John would have had an extremely difficult time in meeting the new standards for a regular high school diploma. He was also accepted into the Air Force and been assigned aircraft mechanic technical school upon completion of his initial recruit training.

Although John is counted as a dropout from public school (a requirement for acceptance into the Commonwealth Challenge Program), he, by all accounts, is a success story, a young person who benefited greatly from the support and intervention of the Student Support Program. John was not meeting with success in the public school system, which caused him to be frustrated. John also suffered from low self-esteem, which was partially the result of his troubled relationship with his birth mother. In a sentence, John had lost hope. The support provided by the Student Support Program, in concert with the caring relationship his resource teacher established with him, helped him regain a sense of hope. As a result, John was able to respond to the structure and rewards he realized in the Commonwealth Challenge Program. Without the Student Support Program, John most likely would not have finished his tenth grade year.

Steve—Persistence Finally Paid Off

It is always difficult to predict who will respond to the assistance that a Student Assistance Program can provide. Steve's is the case of the roller coaster experience of this work. When Steve was referred to me, I felt his level of motivation would be a great asset. I was proved wrong. However, after speaking with his father, I once again was encouraged. Steve's father was very motivated and receptive to a range of suggestions. I was convinced that we would soon see a change in Steve's behavior. Again I was wrong.

Steve was an extremely bright ninth grader who had failed three classes in the seventh grade and one class in the eight grade. His first nine-week grade point average, based on a 4.0 scale, was a 0.83. Steve was referred to me by his Algebra I teacher for his lack of motivation. Steve had scored in the ninety-sixth percentile for his complete composite score on his fourth-grade Iowa Test of Basic Skills (ITBS). On the Stanford 9 test he took in October of his ninth-grade year, he scored above the seventieth percentile on the partial and total battery.

Steve's presenting problem was his lack of attention and low motivation. His math teacher stated that he was gifted when it came to math, but he would never do his homework. He did enjoy doing problems (always correctly) in front of the class at the board. Steve got a D for the first nine weeks in Algebra I.

I had three sessions with him and two lengthy conversations with his father during the first nine weeks, with no progress noted. He knew that he could do better, and stated that he did not like doing so poorly, but nothing changed. I developed a structured plan to monitor his progress, but he seldom did what was asked of him. His father was at a loss to explain his son's lack of motivation. His father was also very frustrated. One of Steve's problems was that he had difficulty being on time to school. I recommended to Steve's father that Steve receive a physical examination. Steve continued to struggle during the second nine weeks, but his father had him tested for attention deficit disorder (ADD), based on the recommendation of his physician. Steve was determined to have ADD and began taking medication during the second nine weeks.

His grades for the second nine weeks improved enough so that he failed only one class. I continued to see Steve and to monitor his progress. Steve was now on-task, sleeping well, and compliant with every recommendation I made. Steve's grades at the end of the third nine weeks were much improved, and he made the honor role for the first time since the fifth grade. His grade point average for the second semester was a 3.2 and final average in Algebra for the fourth nine weeks was a 104!

The medication was central to Steve's change. However, the communication and support that the student support specialist provided was instrumental in the successful outcome. Most likely Steve would have done enough to get by and graduate. His overall grade point average would have been below a 2.0 and the chances that he would ever attend college would have been remote. By the end of this ninth-grade year, he knew what he needed to do to get his grade point average high enough to graduate in the top 20% of his class. He not only had the capacity to do so, but he also now had the motivation.

CONCLUDING REMARKS

The previous five cases exemplify the successes that a Student Support Program can instigate. Many similar examples could have been included. Based on this evidence, it is clear that the need for a program such as this is great in all middle and high schools. I would expect that in most medium-to-large schools the need will most likely exceed what one full-time person can effectively manage.

Of the 141 referrals that I received in one year, progress for some students was more obvious than for others. It is my view that all students benefited, in that they had an opportunity to examine their behavior. Of course, although the change process can be initiated externally, lasting change must also be internal. The Student Support Program gives troubled students an opportunity to substantially change their lives by taking advantage of the external intervention and making a choice to continue the change process. Some students, as evidenced by the five cases, responded in an immediate and obvious manner, but in all cases, seeds were likely planted that may prove to be helpful at a later time.

The success of the program rests heavily on the premise that one of the functions of a school is to assist in the identification and remediation of (or referral for) obstacles that prevent a student from being successful. An ecological orientation is needed (see McAdams and Foster, this volume). There must also be an acknowledgment from the school leadership and school administration that a substantial percentage of the school population is having difficulty due to personal problems.

A commitment to addressing the psychosocial problems of youth is required. It is important for the school and all stakeholders to assist in the identification and remediation of these "nonschool" problems. School leaders must acknowledge that the school is in an excellent position to respond to the most disruptive or difficult students in a proactive manner, before the greater society must respond in a reactive way. These students too deserve to be provided an education just as those who have other special needs or who are gifted or who play sports or have musical talents. It is not a difficult task to show that money expended on an effective Student Support Program is consistent with the goal of excellence in schools. A Student Support Program is a proactive response— instead of simply reacting to disruptive behavior and tolerating or ignoring substandard academic performance, an effective Student Support Program represents an ethical commitment to providing all students with a full life education.

REFERENCE

Anderson, G.L. (1988). *When chemicals come to school.* Greenfield, WI: Community Resource Press.

9

Educating Troubled Youth in Alternative Settings

Karen H. Loy and Dennis E. Gregory

An alternative school can be described as a specialized educational program, one that takes place outside of the mainstream school (Cox, 1999). It is designed to serve students who disrupt their school environment to the point that they are excluded from the environment by means of suspension or expulsion.

American alternative schools have historically been designed to be an option to traditional public school educational settings for students who do not fit the mainstream educational system. During the late 1960s and 1970s, these schools often provided a "free" curriculum, an unstructured school day, and academic freedom for teachers and students. They were also characterized by an experimental and progressive environment. Their student population consisted of students who were alienated, disengaged, or who could not or would not succeed in the mainstream of public education.

CURRENT TRENDS

Disruptive Students

In today's public school environment, these alternative schools have evolved a new dimension. Many districts are pressured by their constituents (faculty, parents, community, and students) to remove disruptive and potentially violent students from the regular school environment and place them in alternative settings. As a result, some of the flexibility originally available in these schools has disappeared, due to the need for students who disrupt their own learning or the learning of others to be educated in these alternative settings. The Federal Office of Juvenile Justice and Delinquency Prevention first suggested that alternative programs be used as a strategy for working with delinquent youth in the late 1980s (Gottredson, 1987). As a result, many alternative schools have become disciplinary schools: the placement of choice for disruptive, defiant rule breakers. As principals in mainstream schools continue to use the exclusion of students as a primary choice of discipline, the alternative school will become increasingly necessary as the disciplinary model of the American educational landscape.

One-Time Offenders

In addition to removing students with a pattern of discipline problems from the mainstream school settings, some districts choose to use the alternative setting to educate one-time offenders: students who commit so-called "zero tolerance" offenses. Some districts desire to educate these students in a special school setting rather than to remove them entirely from the system. Doyle, in this volume, discusses the other option, that is, of school districts choosing to expel and legally deny some one-time offenders all educational services. We consider such expulsion to be an undesirable and destructive method of dealing with difficult students.

Disabled Students

Luckily, the same expulsion option is not allowed for disabled students. The 1997 Amendments to the Individuals with Disabilities Education Act (IDEA) (hereafter IDEA 97) limits the decision-making power of school districts concerning students who are protected as eligible students. IDEA-eligible students cannot be expelled from school with no services. These students' Individual Education Plans (IEPs) must be implemented, and the school district must provide a setting in which this can take place. Alternative schools are often used as the placement of choice for students who are identified as "handicapped" under IDEA 97, when they are disciplined by suspensions or expulsions. These schools are seen as a means for providing the special education students with "free and appropriate public education," regardless of their offenses. The choice of total exclusion for these students is not an option.

Preponderance of Poor and Minority Students

Recent research data have clearly described the students who are placed in, or referred to, alternative schools in our country. The descriptions do not appear complementary to the current norms of inclusion and cultural sensitivity that are valued in the "regular" public school settings. Nor do they support the profession's tenets that "all students can learn" and "high standards for everyone." In fact, many alternative schools have become a place of segregation for the poor and minority students in school districts across our country (Wu, 1980).

Although such separation is certainly problematic, the issue of which students are to be placed in alternative settings is beyond the scope of this chapter. Instead, we address the importance of making alternative schools educationally competitive with mainstream education so that they might best serve the students who are so quickly excluded from that mainstream. This chapter provides a model for the creation of a safe alternative school setting. It describes the elements that these authors believe must be necessary in order for a "culture" of safety to be achieved.

A CULTURE OF SAFETY: APPLYING MASLOW'S HIERARCHY TO ALTERNATIVE SCHOOLS

A culture of safety, or nurturing, is important in providing an alternative educational program for troubled students. Green's (1987) research showed that nurturing could have a positive impact on discipline, attendance and achievement. Nurturing schools are schools that meet the needs of individual students, that is, they are student-centered schools. "Safety" for troubled students takes on a meaning that is somewhat unique, but actually reflects a common human need.

Maslow's hierarchy of needs can be applied in the alternative school setting (Ediger, 1998). Maslow's hierarchy begins with basic physiological needs such as hunger, thirst, and sleep. It then progresses to the next level of needs within which are safety needs. These can include both physical and emotional safety. The third level of Maslow's hierarchy addresses belonging and love. A safe academic environment creates a feeling of belonging for the student. Finally, Maslow's hierarchy includes esteem needs such as self-esteem and the belief that others see and trust a student's ability to succeed socially and academically.

The material that follows examines how the alternative school may help students to achieve needs at each level of Maslow's hierarchy. Although Maslow described safety as only one level of need, the authors have chosen to use the term "culture of safety" to describe the broad setting that allows the alternative school to meet needs at all levels of Maslow's hierarchy.

HUMAN NEEDS AND SCHOOLING

Physiological Needs

The education system as a whole begins to meet the physiological needs of students. This is achieved with the provision of federally funded breakfasts and lunches, as well as school health programs. This is particularly important in alternative school settings due to the large number of economically deprived and minority students. In addition, because these students have a higher than normal level of violence and disruption in their lives outside of school, the provision of services that meets basic physiological needs allows them to control their behavior more easily.

Safety

Although basic physiological needs are met in alternative school settings, physical safety needs, belonging needs, and esteem needs are a more central focus.

Physical Safety

Many students come to school with no thought about their physical safety. They live in safe neighborhoods and in safe families. Many of the troubled students in alternative schools experience just the opposite. Their communities and homes may be unsafe for them. They enter the doors of schools with their defenses up. They must; this is the life they lead.

Belonging

As noted earlier, Maslow's third level of basic needs deals with the area of belonging and love. This level clearly correlates with the emotional safety that is required for troubled students in alternative schools. Affection, intimacy, and belonging have their roots in relationships.

Esteem

The next level of Maslow's hierarchy is esteem needs. There can be another dimension of "safety" for students. They may have a perfectly safe physical environment outside of school, but the environment inside is not safe for them. Schools may present a great danger to their self-worth and self-esteem. Failure in the school environment may produce greater danger than any environment outside of the school. The alternative school setting must produce both a physically safe environment and a psychologically safe environment, one in which students can work through emotional issues and learn without the loss of self-worth.

An "educationally safe" environment is one that allows students to achieve competencies in small groups, increases students' self-esteem, and shows students that their small victories are valued by others. At this level, students gain self-respect, a sense of adequacy, and a level of competency. For six- to eighteen-year-old students, educational success is central to their sense of competency, that is, their self-esteem.

CREATING A CLIMATE OF SAFETY

The alternative schools must create a climate within their boundaries that provides an overall culture of safety: environmental safety, emotional safety, and educational safety. That culture of safety can be the instrument through which the needs described earlier can be met. In climate terms, the school is no longer approached as a machine that is, on the one hand, fixed and working, or conversely, broken and in need of repair. Rather the school is a living organism that moves and changes as its members or parts move and change. A school's climate is the collective set of attitudes, beliefs, and behaviors in a building.

In an alternative school for troubled youth, a climate of safety is imperative. How does the school feel? What are the values and beliefs of the school? How does the school treat its members? As noted previously, three aspects of safety must exist for the school to experience safety in a meaningful way.

Environmental Safety

Whenever a group of students is brought together who have in common that they have recently been rejected by others, have a history of making negative social decisions, and have a tendency to commit violent acts, the mix can be volatile. People with all these characteristics might instead be called a "mob." When a mix of students such as these are placed together, the results could be disastrous, even deadly. Instead, school districts across the country must turn this into a positive group, a learning community, typically in the form of an alternative school. With appropriate considerations, the mix can be dynamic.

Safety in the school environment must be paramount for this dynamism to be productive. Maslow's first and second levels of basic human needs are imperative as we consider this area as part of a larger culture. The consideration of environmental safety is the starting point in this effort. The faculty and students need this safety in order to fulfill their respective roles within the school setting and to create a program that meets their individual needs. Educators must accept that we cannot control people; we can only control the environment.

Important considerations for environmental safety should be made. Included among these are the following.

1. A low adult to student ratio in the classroom should be maintained, as low as one to five

In addition to teachers, paraprofessionals should be included as a vital dimension of alternative staffing patterns. A teacher with a paraprofessional and ten students appears to be a good mix for environmental safety. The small ratio should be complemented by "engagement." There must not just be adults-in-the-room-with-the-students, but adults involved with their students in both words and actions. Staff in an alternative school rarely has the opportunity to sit behind a desk. Even during times of quiet seat work, staff must be up moving about the room, supervising student activity, prompting, cueing, and calling students back to task if they wander. Such activity decreases the occurrence of acting out behaviors due to academic frustration. Engagement is critical as a part of this process. Teachers and paraprofessionals should share in classroom activities (Finn, 1998).

2. Adult supervision of students at all times is necessary

School rituals such as hall passes, mass class changes, and unsupervised gatherings should be eliminated. Routine tasks, such as bathroom breaks, must be supervised. Adult supervision and involvement is one of the best prevention tactics that can be incorporated into any school setting, not just the alternative setting (Gregg, 1999).

3. A closed campus is necessary

Keeping others off, and keeping students on, the alternative school campus is imperative. A separate school building for the alternative program is helpful, but not necessary. Effective alternative programs can be run as a school-within-a-school; however, having its own space and staff is mandatory (Duke & Griesdorn, 1999).

*4. The physical setting must include areas for time-outs,
cool-downs, verbal processing, and counseling*

A physical area in which students can express their frustrations and, at times, anger, is important. "Time-out" is a positive behavioral intervention. Teaching students who are impulsive and explosive to realize that they are upset and can remove themselves from the negative stimulus may lead to tremendous progress toward self-control and responsibility. Such space would ideally be set up specifically for this procedure, and staff should be trained in proper ways to use this process. Isolation of these areas away from mainstream activities is recommended.

5. Behavioral support staff must be provided

A school resource, security, or police officer in uniform is helpful in establishing safety. This person's role must be carefully defined. The job expectations will be dependent on the officer's status (e.g., whether he/she is an employee of the local law enforcement agency or of the school district). This distinction is vital in determining the limits and legality of the officer's actions. Each school district should consult with their legal counsel to gain a clear understanding of the limits and authority of their officers. In addition, having an individual specified as a "behavioral specialist" is essential. This person's sole responsibility should be to provide behavioral support to the classroom staff. This support may include verbal or physical intervention, counseling with students, and other duties, depending on the population.

*6. Searching students must be a routine part of the school
program*

One of the facts we have gleaned from the incidents of deadly violence that gained national attention in the last decade is that the students involved had histories of possession and use of drugs and/or weapons. In this volume, Clark describes many of the characteristics we have gleaned about the deadly incidents on school campuses. Students who are assigned to alternative schools have often committed so-called "zero tolerance" offenses related to drugs and/or weapons. Given this and other behavioral and self-control issues that bring students to alternative schools, the potential for violence, drugs, or weapons violations is increased. Therefore, conducting a metal detector search upon school entry on a daily basis helps produce a sense of security. As a result, it is much more difficult to get a weapon into the school facility. In areas where street violence is a part of the student's campus life, this safety precaution can eliminate the need for students to feel the need for "equalizers" while at school (Ehrensal, 1996).

7. Video cameras should be used in all common areas and even in every classroom

The use of video surveillance has been shown to be an effective deterrent to crime (Green, 1999). A proviso is in order: Any time video surveillance cameras are used, people who enter the school must be informed. Although this need to inform is important, it could be a cause for self-consciousness. However, after an initial adjustment period most students and staff will forget the camera's presence in the environment. Some students can learn great lessons from watching their own actions on video and having these discussed with them by a trained staff member.

8. Physical intervention training of all staff is necessary

Students with histories of violence and low impulse control in any school setting, and particularly in one such as in an alternative school, may need to be physically controlled. Consequently, strict guidelines for physical intervention strategies must be developed and implemented. Training must be provided for all staff, and desired levels of physical ability should be a requirement for employment. Regular review of physical intervention responses should also be undertaken (CEC, 1996).

Many of these environmental safety precautions do raise important legal issues. Their implementation and continued use must be approved and reviewed by local school boards and central office staff. They must be implemented only after consultation with the school district's legal advisors. Although these measures are recommended and are legal in schools at this time, they may face challenge by parents and student advocates who feel that students' rights have been violated. The legal environment in schools is an evolving entity. As such, constant care for scrutiny is needed.

Emotional Safety

The environmental safety issues are the easiest safety concerns to address. They can be seen in operation and checked for effectiveness of implementation. However, creating an emotionally safe culture within an alternative school is more difficult.

Emotional safety can only come after physical safety is established. An emotionally safe culture is one in which its members are secure that they are heard, that they are valued, that they can contribute, and that they can have their needs met. Emotional safety translates into trusting relationships. Troubled students have a great need to develop relationships with adults (Testerman, 1996). The following beliefs must be in operation for an emotionally safe community to exist for its members.

1. Every voice is important

Students perceiving themselves as important is vital in an alternative setting. Many of these students are disengaged from the educational process. They simply "don't do school." Attendance is poor. Grades are failing. Resistant attitudes are pervasive. But each of these students has a story to tell, and the alternative school staff needs to listen. It is relatively easy to identify what the problems are, but it is far more difficult to understand why the problems exist. Broad categorizations are often quick to be made about the students. However, they have walked individual paths to arrive in the alternative educational setting. Individualized understanding is required for solutions to be achieved (Darling-Hammond, 1997).

2. Meeting basic needs is necessary

Troubled students often have troubled lives outside of school. Students may often bring turbulent issues with them to school. These issues ultimately affect their ability to learn. Serious social issues seem to be magnified in the alternative school setting. Poverty, drug and alcohol use, family dysfunction, physical abuse, sexual abuse, and domestic violence are frequently a part of the troubled student's life. The school has to develop social services to assist these students with their needs for food, clothing, shelter, and safety. Only if students have needs met will alternative schools be able to address more advanced educational needs within the concept of creating a "culture of safety."

We must assist in the resolution of these "imported troubles" if schools are to provide emotional safety. As described earlier, many students in the alternative school setting come to school literally hungry. The federally funded free and reduced lunch program is vital for students who come to school hungry each day. On some days, schools may not serve breakfast or lunch due to a varied time schedule. On these days, practicality must win out, and students may need to be fed by other means. Hungry students do not learn well, but, more important, knowing someone is hungry and not feeding them is morally and ethically wrong. Doyle, in this volume, describes the flexibility that can be brought into play in order to have effective schools.

3. Crisis is an opportunity to learn

In these special schools that are designed for students who have frequently made "poor decisions," crises based upon bad judgment will occur. Students will inevitably fight. Students will argue. Students will be defiant. However, instead of viewing a crisis as simply a change in the equilibrium or status quo that simply must be controlled, it must be viewed as providing a teachable moment. A crisis occurs whenever a student runs out of, or has never learned, adequate ways of coping when faced with stressful, hurtful, or undesirable situations (Holden, Mooney, & Wells, 1993). A crisis must not be viewed only as a challenge to authority, but rather as an opportunity for the student to learn a new skill. One method to achieve this learning lies in the so-called "Life Space Crisis Interviews." This protocol for working with students in crisis is a tool for facilitating the crisis-to-opportunity process (Long & Morse, 1996). The emphasis in these interviews lies in listening to the student's viewpoint. Nothing shows students that they are valued as much as active listening does.

4. Empower others to "own" their decisions

Schools are a system of power structures. In alternative school settings, power structures must be realized and applied. Three kinds of power have been described as available in organizations: coercive power, remunerative power, and normative power (Etzioni, 1975). Coercive power rests on the application or the threat of physical sanctions: infliction of pain, restriction of movement, and control of basic needs. Remunerative power rests on the control over material resources used as rewards such as salaries, trophies, and services. Normative power rests on the allocation of symbolic rewards, for example, esteem, prestige, and placement.

Coercive power is the least effective power. It relies on force. The victim says, "I will do what you ask, because you can make me." Unfortunately, the typical school often operates as if it has a large amount of this power. Although this power does exist, there is very little any of us can actually make someone do. Alternative schools must develop rewards and natural consequences in all aspects of the school environment; that is, they must emphasize remunerative power. Many things can be rewards. The receiver of such rewards will think, "I will do what you ask, because I want what you have to offer." However, this is not where students should remain, and schools must support students' moves to the next level. The ultimate goal should be for students to learn to operate in the area of normative power. "I will do what you ask, because it is the right thing to do." Moral development occurs at this point to a conventional or "conscience" level (Kohlberg & Hersh, 1977).

5. Behavior is learned

Teaching positive social skills must be a part of the curriculum for an alternative school. Many social skills curricula available in the commercial market are thought provoking and interesting to today's student. Emphasis should typically be placed on decision-making skills and anger management. A time should be set aside each day for actual cognitive social skills instruction. However, this formal instruction is not sufficient. Positive social skills have to be integrated into every aspect of the school day. The skills that are valued must be reinforced repeatedly in the education milieu. The school must take this "hidden curriculum" that is concealed in the everyday school setting and make it explicit to the alternative student. The environment must be positive and reinforcing for the students.

6. Behavior is relational

Building relationships is the most common sense approach to behavior management. People change their behaviors for the people around them. Everyone can identify behaviors (actions) he or she will engage in with their family, their children, and their partner that they will not engage in with anyone else. Relationships are important in the governance of actions. Young people are actually looking for significant adult relationships, no matter how tough or resistant the student may seem to be. Forming a significant relationship with a new student should always be a priority. The troubled student will first change his or her negative behaviors for a specific person and then generalize the behavioral changes to others. Often when a student continues to have behavioral difficulties in the alternative setting, it is discovered that no adult has a significant relationship with the student.

7. Behavior is predictable

Human behavior can be predictable. The Individuals with Disabilities Education Act (1997), a federal law, requires the development of "functional behavioral assessments" (FBAs) and corresponding "behavioral intervention plans" for disabled students whose behaviors interfere with their learning or the learning of others (both are described in chapter 2 of this volume). An important premise of the functional behavioral assessment is understanding the conditions in which the problem behavior occurs. The following questions are asked in the FBAs: When does the behavior occur? What happens just before the problem behavior? What happens just after the problem behavior? Where does the behavior occur?

With whom does the problem behavior occur? The converse of each of these questions is important as well. School staff must examine the conditions of a student's problem behavior to predict when the behavior will occur. That assessment will assist the school staff in changing the problem behavior into a positive social behavior.

The key to creating a context for emotional safety is to create an environment in which individual psychosocial needs in the at-risk students who come to an alternative school environment are recognized. Building this component of an overall culture of safety focuses on meeting basic needs and then using each experience to develop emotional growth.

Educational Safety

The last level of the safety culture is educational safety. The concept of educational safety assumes that in the right environment all students can learn. Learning is a risky undertaking for most troubled students. Many have disengaged themselves from learning due to their multiple failures in the classroom. For some students it may be the first time in their educational life that they are in a safe learning environment.

The reform movements that are affecting our national educational environment can be applied specifically to the alternative school as well. The notion of creating "effective schools" should be applied to those schools that educate troubled students, as well as the "standard" ones. Current trends in standards development, teacher accountability, brain research, learning styles, and teacher effectiveness should be applied here as in other schools.

Until recently, most research indicated that schools make little difference in student achievement outcomes in comparison to the influence of family background characteristics. However, the most recent findings show that schools can make a difference in student achievement regardless of the community in which the school resides. The most important factor is what goes on inside the school that impacts student learning (Payzant & Gardner, 1994; Phi Delta Kappan, 1988; Odgen & Germinario, 1994). Principals and teachers make the difference in the achievement of students. The adults closest to student learning influence that learning the most. Students from impoverished homes and communities can reach academic benchmarks, as can students with emotional and other difficulties. The educationally safe environment is created and maintained by primarily two classes of staff—principals and teachers.

1. Principals must be effective leaders

The principal of an alternative school must be an instructional leader. Instructional standards must be set for the faculty. The principal should also set learning standards for the students. The school leader must be a coach and cheerleader for effective instruction by the faculty and high achievement for all students. A learning/teaching environment must exist for all stakeholders in the school. Each participant must see learning as his or her own responsibility and have decision-making power and ownership of his or her learning opportunities. Even low-achieving students must be empowered by principals to learn for themselves. The school leader must set achievement benchmarks. He or she must then reward student achievement. People reinforce what they value. The educationally safe learning culture is one that is created by the school leader who provides the materials, the resources, the environment, and the rewards through which students and faculty can take the risks to learn.

2. Teachers must influence the learning environment

The classroom teacher is the single most powerful influence on student learning. The conditions that exist behind the closed classroom door will directly determine the level of student achievement. The educationally safe environment must be one that accounts for student learning styles and allows teachers the flexibility to work with student's individual learning styles. Teachers must view students from the perspective of students' personal strengths. Teachers must probe to discover students' interests in learning. They must capitalize on the students' backgrounds and experiences. Student learning must be personalized and made relevant. Effective instruction must be the goal of every teacher. Curriculum must be aligned with instruction and assessment.

Brookover, Erickson, and McEnvoy (1997) include six characteristics of effective instruction:

A. *All students' learning must be for mastery.* This criterion must be used to provide organization, structure, and goal setting in the classroom. The mastery approach requires a high level of teacher creativity and assessment. If students are not learning, instruction must change. Accurate assessment must validate student learning.

B. *Direct instruction is a crucial element of introducing new skills and new materials.* Effective direct instruction involves keying into student learning styles and using cognitive structuring to prepare the students to learn. Direct instruction includes whole-class presentation and controlled practices.

C. *Time-on-task must be monitored and required for all students.* Students being distracted is taboo in the effective classroom. An age-old adage suggests that the best way to decrease acting-out behavior is to increase time-on-task. Research reveals a close relationship between students' time engaged in learning activities and their level of academic achievement (Chick, 1992).

D. *Effective teachers must use appropriate discipline and classroom management strategies in their classrooms.* Discipline can be contrasted to classroom management. "Discipline" is the teacher's reaction to inappropriate student behavior. "Classroom management" represents the teacher's actions to prevent student misbehavior. It includes teacher-directed planning, managing, and monitoring of student learning activities and behavior problems. Effective instructional planning is a key to effective classroom management. Students who are academically frustrated are frequently the students with behavior problems. Appropriate assessment and instruction are crucial. To use a sports analogy, "the best defense is a good offense." Attention to preventing problem behaviors in the classroom is where efforts should be concentrated.

E. *Effective teachers use cooperative mastery learning opportunities to enhance student achievement.* Cooperative learning activities produce highly motivated students. This strategy harnesses the power of the entire class to participate in active learning. Such activity and involvement contrast to using the power of a single teacher's efforts in passive learning. Capturing students' power to create their own positive learning experiences can be energizing for any teacher. Cooperative learning opportunities also facilitate student-to-student relationships. Increasing the number of student friendships is positively associated with increasing achievement (Vandell & Hembree, 1994).

F. *Appropriate reinforcement should be used.* Teachers must reinforce the behaviors that they value in the classroom. Rewards must include both tangible and social reinforcers. Rewards must move from extrinsic to intrinsic to ensure that the desired behaviors are generalized. Effective teachers should reinforce academic performance, academic effort, prosocial skills, cooperation, teacher-pleasing behaviors, rule compliance, and work habits. Teachers must first clearly communicate what student behaviors are expected. Second, teachers must show by their actions (rewards) that they value these same behaviors. Effective teaching strategies are a necessary part of producing an educationally safe environment. That environment will produce student learning.

CONCLUSION

Linda Darling-Hammond describes in her book *The Right to Learn* (1997) the optimal conditions for safety and caring:

Relationships matter for learning. Students' trust in their teachers helps them develop the commitment and motivation needed to tackle challenging learning tasks. Teachers' connections to and understanding of their students help those students develop the commitment and capacity to surmount the hurdles that accompany ambitious learning. Key to teacher-student connections are continuing relationships and mutual respect, conditions best supported in small school units. (p. 134)

This description could just as aptly characterize the effective alternative school program. It must be the ultimate system of care.

The alternative school has evolved from its early days as program through which unmotivated learners were coached to improve their skills and attitudes by means of small group instruction to a broader effort through which the most difficult and often dangerous students can be motivated to believe in themselves as learners. It does so by first of all providing a climate of safety, as described in this chapter. Students come to the alternative school with many types of disabilities, with backgrounds that make learning an unpopular and often dangerous endeavor, with needs that are not being met at home or in other school settings, and with all of the other needs typical to young people. Few believe in themselves as learners. This chapter has provided a template that can assist teachers, principals, and other school staff to meet the essential and foundational needs of these students. We hope that our recommendations will provide programmatic ideas and inspiration for school districts, alternative school leaders, and alternative school teachers to truly educate the most troubled youth in our society.

REFERENCES

Brookover, W.B., Erickson, F.J., & McEnvoy, A.W. (1997). *Creating effective schools* (2nd Ed.). Holmes Beach, FL: Learning Publications.

CEC Policy on Physical Intervention (1996). Reston, VA: Council for Exceptional Children (ERIC Document Reproduction Service No. 400 634).

Chick, J.J. (1992). *Snapshot #22, using school time productively* (School Improvement Research Series). Portland, OR: Northwest Regional Educational Laboratory.

Cox, S.M. (August, 1999). An assessment of an alternative education program for delinquent youth. *Journal of Research in Crime and Delinquency, 36,* 323–336.

Darling-Hammond, L. (1997). *The right to learn.* San Francisco, CA: Jossey-Bass Publishers.

Duke, D.L., & Griesdorn, J. (1999). Considerations in the design of alternative schools. *Clearing House, 73,* 89–92.

Ediger, M. (1998). *Caring and the elementary curriculum* (ERIC Document Reproduction Service No. ED 422 085).

Ehrensal, P.A. (1996). Mass and intrusive searches of students in public schools: A critical perspective. *Journal for a Just and Caring Education, 2,* 242–255.

Etzioni, A. (1975). *A comparative analysis of complex organizations* (rev. ed.). New York: Macmillan, Free Press.

Finn, J.D. (1998). *Class size and students at risk. What is known? What is next?* Washington, DC: National Institute on the Education of At-Risk Students (ERIC Document Reproduction Service No. ED 418 208).

Gardner, J.W. (1984). *Excellence: Can we be equal and excellent too?* New York: W.W. Norton & Company.

Gottredson, D.C. (1987). Examining the potential delinquency through alternative education. *Today's Delinquent, 6,* 87–100.

Green, M. (1999). *The appropriate and effective use of security technologies in U.S. schools.* Albuquerque, NM: Saudia National Labs (ERIC Document Reproduction Service No. ED 436 943).

Green, R.L. (June, 1987). Nurturing characteristics in schools related to discipline, attendance and eighth grade proficiency test scores. *American Secondary Education, 26,* 7–14.

Gregg, S. (1999). Creating effective alternatives for disruptive students. *Clearing House, 73,* 107–113.

Holden, M.J., Mooney, A.J., & Wells, B. (1993). *Therapeutic crisis intervention trainer's manual.* Ithaca, NY: Family Life Development Center, Cornell University.

Individuals with Disabilities Education Act, Pub. L. No. 105–17, 20 USC § 1400 et seq.

Kohlberg, L., & Hersh, R.H. (1977). Moral development: A review of the theory. *Theory Into Practice, 16* (2), 53–59.

Long, N.J., & Morse, W.C. (Eds.). (1996). *Conflict in the classroom: The education of at-risk and troubled students* (5th ed.). Austin, TX: Pro-Ed.

Odgen, E.H., & Germinario, V. (1994). *The nation's best schools: Blueprints for excellence. Volume I: Elementary and middle schools.* Lancaster, PA: Technomic Publishing.

Payzant, T.W., & Gardner, M. (1994). Changing roles and responsibilities in a restructuring school district. *NAASP Bulletin, 78,* 8–17.

Phi Delta Kappan. (1988). Why do some urban schools succeed? The Phi Delta Kappan study of exceptional urban elementary schools. *Phi Delta Kappan, 77,* 359–363.

Testerman, J. (1996). Holding at-risk students: The secret is one-on-one. *Phi Delta Kappan, 77,* 364–366.

Vandell, D.L., & Hembree, S.E. (1994). Peer social status and friendship: Independent contributions to children's social and academic adjustment. *Merrill-Palmer Quarterly, 40,* 461–477.

Wu, S.C. (1980). *The foundations of student suspensions.* Manoa, HI: Hawaii University (ERIC Document Reproduction Service No. ED 201 054).

10

Creating Computerized Communication Linkages with Parents: The Future Is Now

Frank Scaringello

"Parental involvement is essential to academic success." This axiom has been stated so often that it is considered to be a fundamental truth of education. Studies show that parents who provide a nurturing, positive environment, express high expectations of achievement, and are positive role models increase a student's probability of academic success (Christenson & Conoley, 1992; Hoover-Dempsey & Sandler, 1995; Henry, 1996). When schools provide these same conditions, a powerful synergy exists, one that increases the student's probability of academic and social success.

Despite this seemingly sure-fire formula, it often seems that parents and schools are working in two different worlds, with little coordination. Even with the best of intentions on the part of both families and educators, there is often very little communication between home and school. As mentioned earlier in this volume by Dorries, there are several attitudes among educators that act as barriers to effective school and family linkages. The most significant ones include the belief on the part of school staff members that parents of students from low socioeconomic status (SES) backgrounds place little value on education and the expectation that the student will make the school-family connections. These barriers block the potential school-family connection.

SPECIFIC BARRIERS TO FAMILY-SCHOOL COMMUNICATION

There are several reasons why the family-school partnership has not been effective. First, parent work schedules and schools hours conflict. This phenomenon is especially true in this era of dual working couples or single parents. A solution to this "timing problem" seems to lie in "off hours" interactions. However, those do not happen regularly, as teachers already have significant evening professional and personal commitments: to prepare lesson plans, correct papers, plan instruction, and attend to family and personal needs. Hence, evening calls to parents become another encroachment on a teacher's time and do not occur as frequently as they might otherwise. A second barrier to effective communication lies in the pressure placed on teachers by the national accountability testing movement, sometimes called "Standards of Learning." Under such pressure, teachers must focus their instructional time on doing the most good for the most students. This pressure can result in some students becoming "lost in the shuffle." They are usually the ones who are in the lower academic percentile ranks. It is no wonder that actual, effective parental involvement is such a difficult goal to achieve.

CURRENT METHODS FOR MAKING SCHOOL-FAMILY LINKAGES

Communication today between families and schools relies mostly on old, unwieldy, non-immediate technology: telephone calls, notes, conferences, progress reports, and report cards. The content of the first three means of communication usually tends to be problem focused and reactive, and usually carries the assumption that the student is not performing up to par. As parents of a school-age child can attest, how often does the teacher call at night to congratulate the parent on their child's excellent performance?

It need not be so unwieldy nor reactive. In the latter case, there are some well-established proactive measures for communicating with families, such as newsletters, homework hotlines, and Parent-Teacher Association meetings. Although these represent earnest attempts at interaction between parents and schools, they suffer from methods that make linkage ineffective or, in effect, nonexistent. In each of the current communication methods, there is a long lag time between message initiation and delivery to the audience. In contrast to this situation, it is known that timely feedback to students by parents reinforces positive student behavior and can correct problems before they escalate (Duty, 1997). The current communication vehicles that are in common use do not offer such a desirable fast turn-around time. They make limited use of available state-of-the-art technology. In practice, we are still left with the isolated school and isolated family, especially for students whose families are poorer and less schooled. And it does not have to be so.

THE FUTURE OF FAMILY-SCHOOL COMMUNICATION

All the necessary technology for immediate, proactive communication between families and schools is available now. In the past ten years, electronic mail has become pervasive. The availability of the Internet, and the information on it, has reached a saturation point. Computers are in workplaces, religious buildings, recreation centers, libraries, and homes. It therefore makes sense that some schools should start to use cyberspace to communicate with their clientele. However, this author's perusal of the Web sites of three private schools and twelve school districts revealed that most school Web pages were static and were merely informational. Only one of them listed current homework assignments. These Web pages displayed anywhere from too little to too much information, and all of it was static material. Most often listed were superintendent biographies, Standards of Learning results, district vision and goals, and school vicinity maps. Such information usually has a one-time use. What is needed is a dynamic, interactive vehicle for two-way communication between the school and family. What I have called a "Cyber-Linkages Model" can be that vehicle.

A CYBER-LINKAGES MODEL FOR SCHOOL-FAMILY COMMUNICATION

This Cyber-Linkages Model (CLM) is a positive response to the question: If parental involvement is important to academic success, how can we provide the most timely, accessible means of communication between parents and educators? The CLM is a dynamic information tool which would enable families and schools to communicate with each other with quick response time. It would provide an up-to-date status of the student's progress, schoolwork, and a means to e-mail the teacher.

An outline of this dynamic electronic communication model follows. It can be applied to all levels of schooling. However, a middle school will be selected for the very first application this model, since that is when most parents have to deal with multiple teachers and more afterschool activities. That is also when parents report losing linkages to the school. The CLM would provide not only specific information about a school but also offers detailed information about each student's progress. Here is an illustration of a middle-school electronic communications model.

Illustration of the CLM for Middle School X

The first page of this Cyber-Model Web site would provide general information about the school (address, phone number, photo of building) and routing to different areas of the Web site. Note that guardians could see their child's record book on-line, as well as any notes that the teachers might have offered. This is the only part of the site that has restricted assess; security for this information could be password-protected based on the student identification number.

Here is a mock-up of the typical site.

Welcome to Middle School X
Administration
Extracurricular activities
Guidance
Nurse
Security
Sports
6th grade
7th grade
8th grade

By double clicking on the seventh box, we would then transfer to the Middle School X sixth-grade section.

Welcome to Middle School X 6th grade
Cluster A
Cluster B
Cluster C
Cluster D

By double clicking on Cluster C, we would enter Cluster C's site.

Welcome to Middle School X 6th-grade Cluster C

Communication Skills

Foreign Languages

Math

Science

Social Studies

Music

Physical Education/Health

Field Trips and Special Events

Meet the Teachers

By double clicking on Social Studies, we would enter the Social Studies section.

Welcome to 6th-grade Cluster C Social Studies

Standards of Learning

Syllabus

Homework

To contact the teacher of this class

My child's grade book for this class

References for this year's syllabus

IMPLEMENTING ELECTRONIC COMMUNICATIONS BETWEEN PARENTS AND SCHOOLS

There are some challenges to overcome if schools are to implement this computerized model for home-school communication. Most significantly, it would require a considerable capital investment in computers, infra-structure, and the technical support to bring the schools' electronic com-munication capability up to today's standards. That may not be a reality in an austere fiscal environment. Equal importance lies in the fact that not all families can afford their own personal computer and Internet access. The investment required for a personal computer and Internet access may shut out the very families who need the help most—the low SES families. Although this disparity in need is a concern, creative use of computers with Internet access in community centers, churches, and other places may minimize this limitation.

Implementation of the CLM model requires a new concept of what is expected of a teacher during the workday. Gone would be the days of just one planning period, as maintenance of this type of Web page, answering the mail, and posting the assignments would require a daily investment in time, along with the previously mentioned financial investment. This model suggests that teachers would need either a lighter student load or an assistant to help with these new tasks. However, I would propose that the potential benefits far outweigh the costs.

CONCLUSION

A computerized communication model would provide families with immediate access to the school from the macroview of the principal to the microview of specific subjects. Parents would be able to access this database at their convenience and provide praise, encouragement, and feedback to their children as necessary in a timely manner. Most important, a direct communication link between the family and teacher would be established.

With a computerized communication linkage, parents would have the opportunity to assume a more proactive role in their children's education. With that proactive role comes even greater opportunities for them to enhance their children's education by teaching them organizational skills, reinforcing the learning of the school curriculum, and praising and correcting behavior as required. With this increased family support, schools would be able to focus more on curriculum delivery and efficacy. It would be a win-win situation for all.

REFERENCES

Christenson, S.L., & Conoley, J.C. (1992). *Home-school collaboration: Enhancing children's academic and social competence.* Silver Spring, MD: National Association of School Psychologists.

Duty, M.J. (1997). *School, family, and community.* Gaithesburg, MD: Asper Publishers.

Henry, M. (1996). *Parent-school collaboration.* Albany: State University of New York (SUNY) Press.

Hoover-Dempsey, K.V., & Sandler, H.M. (1995). Parental involvement in children's education: Why does it make a difference? *Teachers College Record, 95*, 310–331.

11

Bridging the Separation of Church and School through the "Faith in School" Project

Rivers Taylor and Garrett McAuliffe

Many urban schools loom ominously above the city streets. Such it is with the local middle school of which we write. It is an imposing five-story structure, accessible only by means of a steep set of stone steps. A moatlike expanse of grass and shrubs surrounds the school and keeps it apart from the hurly-burly of the gentrified district of cafés and craft shops that surround it. The school is apart from the neighborhood.

This symbolic separation can represent the barriers for parents and students to accessing their schools. In this particular case, there are more barriers. As is typical of many urban schools, this one largely draws from two populations: one majority and relatively affluent; the other minority and relatively nonaffluent. The second group experiences great separation from the school, as the parent organizations and other activities are dominated by the more affluent majority group. The school culture is "foreign" for many members of this community, in language, style, and behavior, perhaps like the plantation house was to the other residents of a community of another time. The separations become vivid when signal events such as honor roll assemblies and orchestra recitals are held. The affluent majority, both parents and students, dominates both activities.

A socially critical eye cannot avoid the disparity. Such an eye might look further, to the outlying neighborhoods that draw the students to this partic-

ular school. The minority neighborhoods are literally across the tracks
from this school building. The gentrified majority neighborhood surrounds
it. This status quo means that the school would, as things stood, inevitably
serve the majority more fully than the outlying minority students—unless a
crisis occurred. Such a crisis triggered the initiative that we describe here.

This chapter is the story of a socially critical response to disparity. It is a
tale of response and action, and success in supplementing the "official" system of school with a grassroots initiative that has blossomed into a model
for school-community linkage. We call it the "Faith in School" project.
There generally must be two central players in the success of an initiative
such as this: activist concerned parents and responsive school system personnel. Both players were present in this case.

IN THE BEGINNING: THE INITIAL IMPULSE

In the current situation, the crisis consisted of growing parental recognition and speaking out about two issues that are common for minority students. First, these students had generally low standardized test scores and a
preponderance of classroom failures. Second, many parents felt that there
was unfair treatment in the way discipline was dispensed, with minority
students receiving inordinately harsher treatment.

Beginning Steps: A Messiah Appears

Members of the minority community expressed these concerns informally in a safe environment: their local church in one of the minority
neighborhood. One particular parent of a former student heard these rumblings at church. She served as a catalyst and organizer for the conversa-
tion. She formed a committee that took these concerns to the pastor of the
church. This parent identified with the pain that this group was feeling because she herself was a survivor of the struggle to educate children in an
alienating environment. With support from her pastor, she went to the
school and to the central administration office for help. She received a very
positive response from key players in the school system, in the person of the
local middle-school principal. They faced the disparity head-on.

And the Word Is Spread: The Conversation Begins

The first collaborative meeting was held at the church and was attended
by both school staff and the local community. This meeting was not a
churchlike "holding and singing hymns service," but, to the contrary, it was

quite confrontive. Feelings ran high. But so did listening. The parents were frustrated and angry because they felt the school staff were not concerned with their needs. In turn, school staff were disappointed with the parental support they were receiving from the minority community. The dialogue was sincere and candid.

Planning and Follow-up

The concerns were noted. All participants agreed that these issues required further investigation and planning. Following this most successful and inspiring meeting, the principal (who is a majority group member herself) and her staff went back to their building and brainstormed ways to implement solutions to the two major problems. The principal assigned a staff member to work closely with the community to bring about change. The first author was that staff member for the middle school. The woman who initially acted on the rumblings was appointed the liaison between the school and the church for community students from grades K to 12.

These four, the church liaison person, the director of counseling for the school (i.e, the first author here), the school principal, and the pastor of the church, together developed a plan for a community event for the following fall semester. A workshop on career and higher education opportunities in the region would be held. Administrators from all of the local school systems and local colleges would be invited to the event. Partnerships would be solicited from area businesses.

The First Faith in School Workshop

The initial activity consisted of holding a "Success Fair" at the church. We, the committee, advertised these meetings by sending out announcements by letter from the school, making announcements at the church, and passing out flyers in the neighborhoods. The workshop highlighted three issues: test taking, career issues, and health matters. We saw it as critical to empower parents with the knowledge necessary for producing a healthy child who can develop into a productive citizen. To do so requires variously addressing academics, emotions, social skills, and spiritual development. For those purposes, we recruited the services of local registered nurses, counselors, teachers, pastors, business people, and higher education staff.

We addressed the particular problem of low test scores by giving parents some strategies to improve test-taking skills. We distributed a handout on "Test Taking Hints," including strategies used before, during, and upon completion of all tests. Corresponding transparencies that illuminated effective test-taking methods were also used.

We decided that a career dimension was needed to address many youths' low motivation and pessimism about the future. For the sake of linking school with the world of careers, we had booths set up to highlight various occupations and future schooling opportunities. College representatives and local businesses set up booths and conducted presentations about the nature of their organization and opportunities in it for the local community. At the booths were community role models in the fields of medicine, engineering, education, business entrepreneurship, and computer-related areas. We had information available from some of the local colleges and universities about scholarships, entrance requirements, and curriculum expectations. Also available at this workshop were materials on vaccines needed for prenatal and preschool care.

The Second Workshop: The Seed Takes Root

The first workshop was well attended and highly successful, as evidenced by the overwhelming response of the participants through letters and telephone calls sent to the superintendent of schools. Inspired by the response to the first initative, we organized a similar but expanded seminar at the church during the winter. We included the same presenters as listed earlier. There we also had motivational speakers, followed by question and answer sessions. The guests addressed additional issues, such as self-esteem, assertiveness, self-discipline, goal setting, and peer pressure.

An unexpected outcome of these sessions lay in a direct and surprising impact on the parents themselves: Because of the information received from these sessions, some of the parents found a new career interest of their own and have gone back to college. Such is the power of such initiatives and the hunger of people for resources and support.

IMPACTS AND CONCLUSION

As a result of the actions of one energized mother who answered the call of distress from her peers, and the active response of concerned parents, community members, and a school staff, a program of school-community involvement has been created. The Faith in School Project began with a vision of linking the chains of community, school, and church, chains that had been broken long ago for the minority community. The chain is being rebuilt. The effort must continue, however, to counter the effects of low parental education and historical exclusion from schooling matters in these types of communities.

We have found that overall test scores for the students involved in these activities have increased. Student self-discipline has steadily improved. Minority parental involvement in academic planning and extracurricular activities such as honor roll assemblies, PTA membership, and special programs has increased dramatically. This "divided" urban middle school is slowly becoming everyone's school.

Future possibilities that have been discussed include achieving greater impact at the local elementary school, having an information line that connects school staff with young, single expectant mothers, bringing in even greater participation from community resources, creating a community Web site, facilitating computer access for all, and seeking funding or grants for more workshops.

Instigating such an inspiring chain of activities is not "normal." The activities are not programmed into school board policy. They are not in school staff members' job descriptions. They require a particular internal sense of justice and the willingness to be an activist. Perhaps they are inspired by someone who also modeled these qualities many years ago in another, faraway community of people who also felt left out.

12

Creating a Character to Promote Good Character in Youth: A Model Program

Sherrill Hurwitz

You have brains in your head. You have feet in your shoes. You can steer
yourself any direction you choose. You're on your own. And you know
what you know. And YOU are the [one] who'll decide where to go.
(Dr. Seuss, *Oh the Places You'll Go!* New York: Random House, p. 1.)

"Children develop character by what they see, by what they hear, and by
what they are repeatedly led to do" (Stenson, cited in Forrest, 2000, p. iii).
This is the proposal of James Stenson, a child psychologist, in regard to how
children acquire character. The word "character" is derived from the Greek
word "to mark" or "to engrave." Individuals with "good" character repeatedly display good behavior. In a sense, these habits are marked, or perma-
nently embedded, in individuals. From what we know about moral
development, moral inclinations do seem to be long-term characteristics of
a person (Higgins, Kohlberg, & Power, 1989).

Character, and its attendant traits or virtues, can be influenced by educators (Higgins, Kohlberg, & Power, 1989). For moral development to occur, children must learn to behave with an understanding that is not solely
based on rules. Character traits must actually be internalized. In addition to
being transmitted, one's character traits are also based on experiences that
a person has (California Department of Education, 1999). The model for

character education that is presented here is based on principles of teaching and learning that allow for internalization and long-term retention. Children learn and remember better if they can relate to ideas in a concrete and experiential way.

Character development can start with the very young. It is therefore urgent that good character be promoted in elementary school. Character education might be considered a central part of all education. Schools are prime settings for addressing or preventing psychosocial problems. The school can complement the work of the home or the religion. In some cases, the school must actually counter the problems at home. Character education is one vehicle for such work.

A CHARACTER EDUCATION PROGRAM: "MRS. CARATA TRAITS"

As an elementary school counselor, I saw a need for bringing character education to the children in a unique way. A concrete, interesting, nonthreatening method of teaching was called for, one that would match students' needs. This approach contrasted with abstract recitations of virtues that had been promulgated by the Scouts and some religious groups. My method consisted of creating a grandmotherly character who demonstrated and promoted good character in many ways.

The Initial Impulse

For several years, I had observed an increase in conduct notices and incident referrals in my school. These artifacts gave evidence of a growing number of children who were unable to get along with others. It paralleled a perceived national trend. There appeared to be an increase in disagreements and/or verbal and physical altercations in my particular school. Although the school's conflict mediation program appeared to be of some help, there seemed to be a need for more.

It was in this context that I gave birth to the idea of "Mrs. Carata Traits" (pronounced Care-a-ta Traits). She (i.e., me) dressed as a kindly grandmother figure. I decided that the best way to present character traits was through a figure who represented character. Mrs. Carata Traits is a familial, parental figure. The family is one source of good character traits. Children learn good traits and develop and build their character through reinforcement from the family. Mrs. Carata Traits's grandmotherly appearance makes a positive connection with this family context. The children relate to the grandmother figure and are likely to feel that there is value in what she is saying to them. In this chapter I describe the character education program that Mrs. Carata Traits represents.

Character-Building Activities

Personifying the Sixteen Character Traits

The character of Mrs. Carata Traits engages in a variety of character-building interventions. She gives advice to students. She also tries to help them work out their everyday problems in school and in other domains in their lives. The advice itself is drawn from the sixteen character traits that have been chosen by our local school district. These traits are respect, responsibility, integrity, honesty, perseverance, kindness, manners, work ethic, self-discipline, tolerance, trustworthiness, compassion, hospitality, patience, citizenship, and courage. (See the appendix to the chapter.)

Every week, Mrs. Carata Traits appears on the school's closed-circuit television morning announcements. She introduces the "character word of the week," gives the definition of it, and provides some examples as to how this word relates to the children's everyday situations.

Letters from the Children

On the morning announcements program, Mrs. Carata Traits encourages the children to write to her via the school's "wee-deliver" postal system. In the past two years, she has received over a thousand letters from the children, and she has answered each one with a personal note. An example of the importance of these personal notes lies in the frequency of letters about the in-home abusive situations. It is obvious that some children find it easier to confide in a "pretend person" about a serious situation. I, as Mrs. Carata Traits, then call the children individually into my office, speak with them, and take the necessary actions. While I, as Mrs. Carata Traits, stay in her costume when I am in the classrooms and also when I am on the television, I do not do so when I need to call the students into my office for such serious conversations.

Adding a Musical Dimension

At the end of her weekly appearance on the morning announcements, Mrs. Carata Traits leads the entire school in the singing of the "Character Traits Song," which is a parody written by the author's daughter and sung and recorded by a local rabbi. This repetitive singing of the song helps the children to remember the sixteen traits and serves as one more mode of communication between the students and Mrs. Carata Traits.

Appearances in Other Settings

In addition to this televised session, Mrs. Carata Traits interacts with the children in many other settings: I appear, in character, before and afterschool, during lunch in the cafeteria, at school functions such as "Community Fun Day," and at Parent-Teacher Association (PTA) programs. Another important way that Mrs. Carata Traits communicates with the student body is through classroom guidance. She goes to every classroom in the building with a Mrs. Carata Traits activity booklet. They discuss the traits and play word games found in the booklet.

The "Character Club"

A larger, more sustained effort has also been initiated: A "Character Club" has begun at this local elementary school. The club was created last year and is coordinated by me, as Mrs. Carata Traits. The club consists of fifth-grade students who have previously shown good character. These students served as ambassadors of good character for the rest of the school. Those initial club members have now moved on to middle school. A seed has been planted. We hope that, as a result, good character will continue to grow in them, and it will spread. It is hoped they will continue to be "ambassadors" of good character. We have now moved the "Character Club" to the fourth-grade level. These students will be able to continue this process into their fifth-grade year.

CONCLUSION AND IMPACT

The current need for character education is evident. It has traditionally been a part of what the family did. Character education also needs to be a part of schooling. The overall response to the character of Mrs. Carata Traits and to the program of character education has been very positive. Administrators, parents, teachers, students, and outside consultants give the program glowing reports. For example, our school recently had an on-site visit from a consultant from a national Quality Education Program. He spoke with faculty and staff and also some individual students. It was reported back to me that, when he interviewed one of the students, he asked, "What makes your school special?" The student replied, "We have Mrs. Carata Traits here and that makes us all feel special."

Although we do not have hard data as to the effectiveness of the Mrs. Carata Traits project with the students, we do have anecdotal evidence that since February 1998, when we began this project, the number of children sent to the principal's or the assistant principal's offices for disciplinary action has dropped. In addition, the number of discipline referrals written by the school staff has also been reduced. This apparent impact challenges elementary school counselors and teachers to initiate creative character-building interventions, ones that engage the students and meet them at their developmental levels.

REFERENCES

California Department of Education (1999). *Character education about character education*. http://www.cde.ca.gov/character/aboutpg.

Forrest, D. (2000). *Character under construction*. Chapin, SC: Youth Light, Inc.

Higgins, A., Kohlberg, L., & Power, F.C. (1989). *Lawrence Kohlberg's approach to moral education*. New York: Columbia University Press.

APPENDIX: DEFINITIONS OF THE SIXTEEN CHARACTER TRAITS

Respect: Showing high regard or consideration for self, for others, for property, and for authority. Understanding that people have value as human beings.

Responsibility: Being dependable in carrying out obligations and duties. Showing reliability and consistency in words and conduct. Being accountable for one's own actions.

Integrity: Having the inner strength to be truthful, trustworthy, and honest. Acting justly and honorably. Being true to one's moral and ethical beliefs.

Honesty: Earning or accomplishing something in a fair manner. Carrying out responsibilities carefully and with integrity. Being willing to acknowledge mistakes and tell the truth.

Perserverance: Being persistent in pursuit or worthy goals in spite of difficulty, opposition, or discouragement. Having the fortitude to try again when confronted with delays, mistakes, or failures.

Kindness: Having a high regard for the welfare and interests of others, which compels one to action on their behalf. Doing something nice for others without expecting anything in return.

Manners: Being courteous to others. Showing polite ways of behaving toward others.

Work ethic: Having productive work or study skills and attitude. Demonstrating hard work and commitment to achieving a desired goal.

Self-discipline: Knowing one's responsibilities and carrying them through faithfully without supervision. Being in control of one's words, action, and desires.

Tolerance: Understanding the traditions and customs of people from different ethnic and religious backgrounds.

Trustworthiness: Deserving of trust, honor, and confidence in relationships.

Compassion: Showing sympathetic attitudes toward others in need, together with a desire to help.

Hospitality: Extending a friendly reception or welcome to newcomers or guests. Offering a pleasant and supportive environment to others.

Patience: Having the ability to wait calmly without losing self-control. Showing a calm endurance in a trying or difficult situation.

Citizenship: Recognizing and living up to obligations to society and community. Being committed to active involvement in one's community.

Courage: Having the determination to do the right thing even when others do not; the strength to follow one's conscience rather than the crowd. Having the confidence to attempt difficult things that are worthwhile.

Index

About the Editor and Contributors

Garrett McAuliffe is a faculty member in the Counseling Program at Old Dominion University, a former schoolteacher in New York, and a former community college counselor and administrator in Massachusetts.

Alan A. Arroyo is Dean of the School of Education at Regent University, Virginia Beach, Virginia. His teaching and research have centered on assisting educators in meeting the needs of students who present behavioral and/or academic challenges.

Mark Blagen is an adjunct faculty member in the human services program at Old Dominion University with recent experience designing and piloting a counseling program for at-risk adolescents. He has been a certified substance abuse counselor (CAC) since 1990.

Mary Ann Clark is a faculty member in the department of counselor education at the University of Florida. She has served as a school counselor and administrator for twenty years in both the United States and in overseas schools.

Denyse Dorries is the behavior/moderate disability specialist at the Training and Technical Assistance Center (T/TAC) at The College of William and Mary. She was a school psychologist for over twenty-five years and continues her work with families of students with disabilities in her private practice.

Lynn Doyle is currently a faculty member in the educational leadership program in the Darden College of Education at Old Dominion University in Norfolk, Virginia. She has worked with troubled youth in her roles as a special educator and a public school administrator.

Alan Forrest is a professor in the department of counselor education at Radford University. As a licensed professional counselor, he has clinical, teaching, training, and consultative experience in the areas of substance abuse and addictive disorders.

Victoria A. Foster is a faculty member at The College of William & Mary in the field of counseling. She has been the director of a family counseling clinic and a counselor for at-risk adolescents.

Robert A. Gable, Professor and Eminent Scholar at Old Dominion University, was a special education teacher, principal of two alternative education programs, and on faculty at University of Pittsburgh and Vanderbilt University. He has written extensively on ways to deal with challenging behavior in the schools.

Dennis E. Gregory is a faculty member in, and coordinator of, the higher education Program at Old Dominion University and specializes in educational law. He has also served as a classroom teacher in regular education classrooms as well as in an "alternative school" setting and has served as a university student affairs administrator.

Sherrill Hurwitz is an elementary school counselor in Norfolk, Virginia and a former social worker dealing with adoptions and Child Protective Services.

Karen H. Loy is a public school educator in Knoxville, Tennessee and a doctoral student at the University of Tennessee.

Charles R. McAdams III is a faculty member in counseling at The College of William & Mary. For over twenty years his clinical practice and research have focused on improving clinical and educational services for aggressive youth and other challenging client populations.

Frank Scaringello is a guidance counselor in the Portsmouth, Virginia public school system. Prior to his present position, he spent twenty-two years as a naval officer and NATO coordinator.

George Selig holds the distinguished chair of educational leadership at Regent University in Virginia Beach, Virginia. Previous to that appointment he was provost of the university for eleven years. His research interest is in students who have behavioral and learning difficulties.

Rivers Taylor is Director of Counseling at Blair Middle School in Norfolk, Virginia and pastor at St. Johns Temple in Newport News, Virginia.